The Information Law team at Forbes Solicitors regularly advises schools, colleges, charities and a wide range of public and private sector organisations about data protection law and practice. The team is involved in delivering briefings to education sector events and providing training to school leaders and to staff through shared sessions or in-house.

Their experience of advising schools and supporting Data Protection Officers in their daily responsibilities provides the basis for this book.

For more on Forbes Solicitors' Information Law work see their website at https://www.forbessolicitors.co.uk/business/business-law/gdpr.htm

A Practical Guide to GDPR for Schools

A Practical Guide to GDPR for Schools

Forbes Solicitors

Law Brief Publishing

Published 2019 by Law Brief Publishing, an imprint of Law Brief Publishing Ltd
30 The Parks
Minehead
Somerset
TA24 8BT

www.lawbriefpublishing.com

Paperback: 978-1-912687-75-6

PREFACE

In writing this book, we have set out to provide school specific guidance to assist you with complying with the General Data Protection Regulation (EU) 2016/679 ('the GDPR') as applied by the Data Protection Act 2018, the issues most commonly encountered within a school setting, the issues schools may face internally and the effects compliance may have on a school's relationship with external organisations.

The style which we have adopted has been intended to assist someone with some prior basic knowledge of data protection law to apply this knowledge in a school setting but will hopefully also assist those getting to grips with data protection in schools for the first time. We have included references throughout the book to the relevant parts of legislation, guidance and case law to assist the reader to consult with original source material if they want to undertake further reading into the subject.

This book is a collaborative effort from the Governance, Procurement and Information Team at Forbes Solicitors, with particular thanks to Bethany Paliga for writing the text and to Daniel Milnes for his support, comments and suggestions for improvement. We are also very grateful to Tim Kevan and Garry Wright for their guidance and patience.

The law in this book is that of England and Wales as stated at 1 November 2019 and this book should not be relied upon for the provision of, or as a substitute for, legal advice.

Forbes Solicitors
November 2019

CONTENTS

Introduction		1
Chapter One	Overview	3
Chapter Two	Schools' Obligations under the GDPR	9
Chapter Three	Individuals' Rights under the GDPR	23
Chapter Four	Information Sharing	39
Chapter Five	Data Processors	49
Chapter Six	Emails, Websites and Social Media	55
Chapter Seven	Breaches – Prevention and Mitigation	59
Chapter Eight	Practical Examples & Suggestions	75
Appendix A	Supplier Data Protection Compliance Questionnaire	87
Appendix B	Personal Data Breach Checklist	97

INTRODUCTION

This book is about data protection and specifically how data protection law applies in a school setting. The introduction of the General Data Protection Regulation (EU) 2016/679 ('the GDPR') in May 2018 was the most significant change to European data protection laws in over 20 years. The law introduced greater enforcement powers for our data protection watchdog, the Information Commissioner's Office, and the ability to issue eye-watering fines in response to significant advances in technology and concerns about the erosion of people's privacy.

Whilst the GDPR is very clear about what action can be taken when things go wrong, what is less clear is how it applies in practice. The GDPR applies to a vast variety of organisations, across multiple sectors and throughout the whole of the European Union – it cannot provide specific requirements. What it does is provide a set of data protection principles and rules and leaves the interpretation to individual organisations.

The aim of the book is to provide you with school specific and practical guidance to assist you with complying with GDPR. This book does not set out to cover in detail the entirety of the requirements set out in the legislation and we have focused on areas of particular relevance to schools in order to assist schools in achieving compliance with GDPR based on our experience of advising schools and charities on data protection compliance and providing content used in guidance to the school sector. This book is aimed at school Data Protection Officers and anyone else within an education setting who is tasked with the job of handling data protection requests and compliance with GDPR.

CHAPTER ONE
OVERVIEW

Key Concepts

A number of key concepts will be discussed throughout this book. These terms, taken from the data protection legislation, are fundamental to understanding how data protection law and guidance works. They are:

Data Controller: an individual or an organisation who decides the manner and purpose of how data is processed (e.g. a school as an organisation will be a data controller or in the case of a Multi Academy Trust, the Trust will be the data controller).

Data Processor: an individual or an organisation who processes personal data on behalf of, and under instructions from, the data controller (e.g. a contractor or third-party service provider).

Data Protection Officer (DPO): This is a new statutory job role which was been created by the GDPR and made compulsory for certain organisations. DPOs are responsible for overseeing data protection strategy and implementation to ensure compliance with GDPR requirements.

Data Subject: the living individual whose personal data is processed by either the data controller or data processor or both. In the case of schools, data subjects will include:

- Students
- Members of staff, volunteers, governors or trustees
- Individuals employed by suppliers or third parties who provide outsourced services (e.g. payroll or secure waste disposal)

- Consultants
- Previous members of staff or students

Personal Data: this is information that relates to a living individual who can be identified from that information by itself or with other available information recorded by itself or with other available information. This can include names, initials, ID numbers, job titles and may also include factors specific to an individual's physical, physiological, genetic, mental, economic, cultural or social identity.

Processing: is widely defined and covers anything that can be done with personal data. This includes (but is not limited to):

- Collecting/recording;
- Editing;
- Retaining/storing;
- Organising/structuring;
- Disclosing/sharing;
- Deleting/erasing/destroying/archiving;
- Viewing/listening to; and
- Using to make assessments or decisions.

Special Categories of Personal Data: this is personal data which is sensitive and so requires a greater level of protection. Under the previous Data Protection Act 1998 the equivalent term was "sensitive personal data".

Special categories of personal data are information relating to:

- Racial or ethnic origin;
- Political opinions;
- Religious or philosophical beliefs;

- Trade union membership;
- Genetics;
- Biometrics (such as fingerprints);
- Physical/mental health or condition; or
- Sex life or sexual orientation.

The Information Commissioner's Office (ICO): the UK's independent body set up to uphold information rights. It can provide guidance to individuals and organisations to promote good practice and take enforcement action where there is a breach of data protection legislation.

The GDPR and the DPA 2018

In May 2018, the data protection regime in the UK was overhauled. An EU Regulation known as the General Data Protection Regulation (EU) 2016/679 ('the GDPR') was directly implemented into UK law. Sitting alongside the GDPR, is the Data Protection Act 2018 ('DPA 2018') which supplements the requirements set out in the GDPR and sets out UK-specific exemptions to the GDPR as well as bringing the UK version of the GDPR into UK legislation. Therefore, the two main pieces of data protection legislation which schools must comply with are the GDPR and the DPA 2018.

Data Protection Principles

The GDPR sets out several key data protection principles which schools must comply with when processing personal data[1]. These data protection principles state that personal data must be:

1 Article 5 General Data Protection Regulation (EU) 2016/679

- Processed lawfully, fairly and in a transparent manner ('**the lawfulness, fairness and transparency principle**');
- Collected for specified, explicit and legitimate purposes and not further processed in a manner that is incompatible with those purposes ('**the purpose limitation principle**');
- Adequate, relevant and limited to what is necessary in relation to the purposes for which they are processed ('**the data minimisation principle**');
- Accurate and, where necessary, up to date; every necessary step must be taken to ensure that inaccurate personal data is erased or rectified without delay ('**the accuracy principle**');
- Kept in a form which permits identification of data subjects for no longer than is necessary for the purposes of which the personal data is processed ('**the storage limitation principle**');
- Processed in a manner that ensures appropriate security of the personal data, including protection against unauthorised or unlawful processing and against accidental loss, destruction or damage, using appropriate technical or organisation measures ('**the integrity and confidentiality principle**'); and
- Finally, the school must also be responsible for, and able to demonstrate, compliance with all of these principles ('**the accountability principle**').

The Role of the Information Commissioner's Office

The ICO is the UK's independent body set up to uphold information rights (including rights under data protection legislation, Freedom of Information legislation and Environmental Information regulations).

In terms of data protection, the ICO is responsible for:

- Ensuring organisations use and process personal data in accordance with the law;
- Maintaining a register of ***Data Controllers***;
- Handling concerns or complaints from members of the public and organisations about the use of personal data; and
- Conducting investigations and prosecutions into organisations and individuals that misuse personal data.

The ICO has a number of investigative and enforcement powers it can take against an organisation or an individual for breaching data protection laws. It can:

- Record the fact that there has been a breach of data protection law but take no further action;
- Investigate circumstances surrounding a breach of data protection law and any remedial action that has already been taken;
- Require a ***Data Controller*** to undertake a course of action to prevent further breaches of data protection law;
- Take formal enforcement action turning such a requirement into a legal obligation;
- Conduct onsite assessments including entering premises, accessing documents and interviewing specified persons; and
- Where there is a serious breach of the GDPR, the ICO may serve a monetary penalty notice up to the value of €20 million or 4% of annual global turnover, whichever is higher.

In addition to the formal enforcement powers set out above, action that is taken by the ICO is published on its website and commonly picked up by the media so can have an effect on an organisation's reputation. In addition to action being taken by the ICO, affected individuals now have the opportunity to claims for compensation for distress caused by a personal data breach.

Further discussion of enforcement action by the ICO and consequences of a personal data breach can be found at Chapter 7.

CHAPTER TWO SCHOOLS' OBLIGATIONS UNDER THE GDPR

Applying the GDPR and the DPA in an Education Setting

As the principles of the GDPR and the DPA 2018 are so broad, it can be difficult to determine exactly what obligations schools have when it comes to protecting personal information and compliance with the GDPR.

In order to unpick schools' obligation, the starting point is to keep the '***accountability principle***' in mind. This is the principle in the GDPR which states that ***Data Controllers*** must be responsible for, and be able to demonstrate, compliance with ***the Data Protection Principles***[1] (see 'Data Protection Principles' in Chapter 1 for further details).

Record of Processing Activity

In order to assess a schools' compliance with the GDPR, we advise conducting an information audit or a data mapping exercise to determine and record exactly what personal information the school holds. This involves documenting the following:

- What personal information the school holds;
- The legal basis for holding that information;
- How the information is used;
- Where the personal information came from;
- Where the personal information is stored;

1 Article 5(2) General Data Protection Regulation (EU) 2016/679

- How the personal information is kept safe;
- Who the personal information is shared with; and
- How long the personal information is kept for.

The results of this exercise can then be documented in a record of processing activity (also known as an Information Asset Register). The GDPR requires certain organisations to document their processing activities. This includes organisations with 250 or more employees (e.g. a large multi-academy trust) or organisations that process special category or criminal offence data[2]. Most schools will be obligated by the GDPR to keep a record of processing activity as they will process ***Special Category Personal Data*** (e.g. details of pupils' health and disabilities) and criminal offence data (e.g. by conducting DBS checks during the recruitment process). There is a lot of potential benefit in producing a record of processing even if the obligation to have one does not apply.

Once schools have created their record of processing activity (or Information Asset Register) this will need to be reviewed at regular intervals and updated where necessary.

Legal Bases for Processing Personal Information in an Education Setting

As part of your record of processing activity (or Information Asset Register) you will need to document your legal basis for processing each type of personal information the school has. Any processing of personal information must be done lawfully, fairly and transparently so that it complies with the GDPR[3]. Article 6 of the GDPR sets out 6 different ways in which personal information can be processed lawfully. These are:

---

2 Article 30 General Data Protection Regulation (EU) 2016/679

3 Article 5(1)(a) General Data Protection Regulation (EU) 2016/679

(a) The individual has given you their consent to do so;

(b) It is necessary for the performance of a contract or to enter into a contract with the individual;

(c) It is necessary for compliance with a legal obligation;

(d) It is necessary in order to protect the vital interests of an individual;

(e) It is necessary for the performance of a task carried out in the public interest or in the exercise of official authority vested in the controller; or

(f) It is necessary for the purposes of the legitimate interests of the controller. (This basis is not available to public sector organisations and so may apply to some schools and not others).

In the majority of cases, the schools' legal basis for processing personal information will be as follows:

- it is necessary in order to perform or enter into a contract with an individual (e.g. holding staff bank details in order to facilitate payments to them);
- it is necessary to comply with a legal obligation (e.g. keeping pupils safe and DfE census information);
- it is necessary for the performance of a task in the public interest (e.g. supporting pupil learning and monitoring and reporting on pupil progress); or
- it is necessary to protect vital interests (e.g. information relating to allergies or emergency contact details).

Where you are processing ***Special Category Personal Data*** (such as information relating to health, disabilities or sexuality), the school must have both a lawful basis under Article 6 of the GDPR (as set out above) **and** a lawful basis under Article 9 of the GDPR. We have set out below the lawful bases which will be particularly relevant to schools.

Therefore, you must ensure that one of the following conditions apply (in addition to the conditions listed above):

(a) You have obtained explicit consent from the individual;

(b) It is necessary in order for the school to carry out its obligations under employment, social security or social protection law;

(c) It is necessary to protect the vital interests of an individual who cannot give consent;

(d) The information has already been manifestly made public by the individual concerned;

(e) It is necessary for conducting or defending legal claims;

(f) It is necessary for reasons of substantial public interest (as set out in the DPA 2018[4]);

(g) It is necessary for assessing the working capacity of an employee;

(h) It is necessary for archiving purposes in the public interest.

Once you have established your legal basis for processing personal information this can be documented on your record of processing (or Information Asset Register) so that the school complies with its obligations under the GDPR[5].

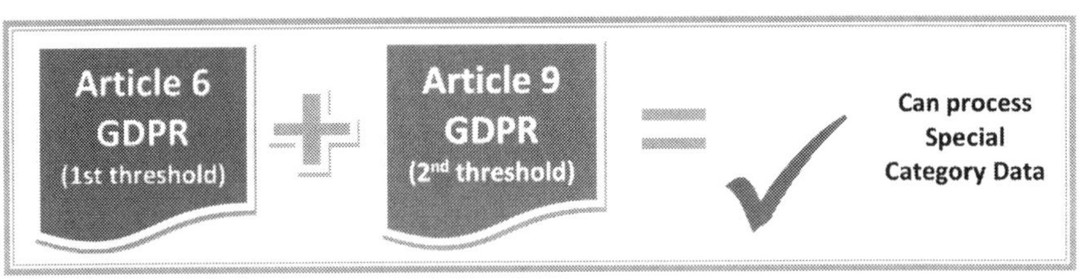

Figure 1. Conditions required for lawful processing of Special Category Data

4 Schedule 1 Part 2 Data Protection Act 2018

5 Article 30 General Data Protection Regulation (EU) 2016/679

Privacy Notices

Once you have conducted your information audit or data mapping exercise, as described above, you will be in a position to prepare privacy notices for the school.

The first data protection principle in the GDPR is to ensure personal information is used lawfully, fairly and transparently. Providing information to individuals about how their details will be used is a key part of demonstrating compliance with this first data protection principle. Additionally, the GDPR is very specific about what information should be provided where personal information is collected from individuals. This is commonly known as a 'privacy notice' or 'fair processing notice'. The GDPR states that the following information must be included in a privacy notice[6]:

- The identity and contact details of the ***Data Controller***;
- The contact details of the Data Protection Officer (where applicable);
- The purposes of the processing for which the personal information is intended to be used and the legal basis for that processing;
- Where applicable, the legitimate interests pursued by the ***Data Controller***;
- Details of who personal information will be shared with;
- Where applicable, the fact that the personal information will be transferred outside of the European Economic Area;
- How long the personal information will be kept for;
- Details of individual rights in relation to access, rectification, erasure, restriction, objection to processing and data portability;

---

6 Article 13 General Data Protection Regulation (EU) 2016/679

- Details of the right to withdraw consent;
- Where applicable, details of the existence of automated decision making including profiling; and
- Details of the right to lodge a complaint with the ICO.

The privacy notice should be provided at the time information is collected (e.g. at the time of enrollment) or earlier if there is earlier engagement such as requesting a prospectus to be sent out or the time at which information about an individual is received by the school from a third party (e.g. applications where the school is involved in assessment using applications lodged with local authority). The privacy notice must be written in clear and plain language which is concise and intelligible, particularly where the information is being collected from a child[7]. This may mean that the school decides to have different privacy notices for parents and pupils. The DfE has produced template privacy notices for schools and has separate privacy notices for parents and pupils as well as an extensive guidance note setting out how schools should approach drafting a privacy notice[8]. In addition to privacy notices for parents and pupils, you should also have a separate privacy notice for your workforce and governors as their information will be used in a different way.

Once your privacy notices have been prepared, they should be reviewed on a regular basis (e.g. annually) to ensure they are still accurate and they should also be updated every time you make a significant change to how you process personal information or introduce new technology (e.g. a new ID system such as fingerprint recognition).

---

7 Article 12(1) General Data Protection Regulation 2016/679

8 Department for Education: Privacy Notices (August 2019)

The Question of Consent

As discussed above, there six different ways to process personal information lawfully. Whilst consent appears first in the list set out in Article 6 of the GDPR, it is the least likely condition to apply and should only be considered where none of the other conditions apply. In a school setting, consent is most likely to be required in the following circumstances:

- To use photographs of pupils for marketing, advertising or on social media;
- To send parents details of fundraising campaigns by text or e-mail;
- To make voluntary referrals to external organisations (e.g. to sign a pupil up to external music or foreign language lessons); and
- To use a biometric recognition system (e.g. to use fingerprints to pay for school meals or to take out library books). This is an example of consent-based processing of ***Special Category Personal Data.***

It is important to note at this stage that under the GDPR, consent only relates to processing personal information. GDPR consent is different to consent relating to medical treatment, participation in events or school educational visits. These consents remain unchanged and are not affected by the GDPR although you should remember that records of those other consents will be the personal information of the individuals giving the consents and the children to which they relate.

Consent should only be used as a lawful basis for processing where none of the other conditions apply as there are a number of practical implications which making using consent an unreliable lawful basis for processing. The GDPR set the bar to obtaining valid consent very high. The GDPR defines consent as:

> "*....any freely given, specific, informed and unambiguous indication of the data subject's wishes by which he or she, by a statement or by a clear affirmative action, signifies agreement to the processing of personal data relating to him or her.*[9]"

This means that consent must be voluntarily given and it must be possible to withdraw consent at any time, which is why consent is an unreliable lawful basis for processing.

The age of a pupil will also be a consideration when determining if consent can be validly obtained. This will depend on whether or not the pupil has the capacity to understand the implications of the processing of their personal information. If they lack capacity to understand this then consent should be obtained by the pupil's parent or carer on their behalf. The general rule in the UK is whether the individual child has the competence to understand and consent for themselves (the 'Gillick competence test[10]') and is generally considered to be around age 12 but will depend on each individual child[11].

Where children's information is being used to offer an online service (e.g. a third-party interactive learning system) directly to a child, there are additional safeguards in the GDPR[12] and the age of consent is set at 13 years old[13]. However, if the online service is only being offered through an intermediary (e.g. only being offered through the school) it is not caught by the additional safeguards in the GDPR as it is not being offered directly to a child[14].

---

9 Article 4(11) General Data Protection Regulation (EU) 2016/679

10 Based on a case about the age at which children can consent to medical treatment without parental consent (Gillick v West Norfolk and Wisbech AHA [1986] AC 112)

11 https://ico.org.uk/for-organisations/guide-to-data-protection/guide-to-the-general-data-protection-regulation-gdpr/consent/what-is-valid-consent/#what8

12 Article 8 General Data Protection Regulation (EU) 2016/679

13 Section 9 Data Protection Act 2018

Finally, it is important to note that consent does not last forever and should be reviewed and refreshed at regular intervals. Consent given by a parent or a carer on a child's behalf will not automatically expire when the child reaches the age at which they could consent themselves, but this is something that should be considered when consent is being reviewed and refreshed[15].

Data Protection Officers

One of the big changes by the GDPR was the introduction of the requirement to appoint a ***Data Protection Officer (DPO)*** in certain circumstances to oversee an organisation's data protection compliance.

Who Needs One?

Not every organisation is required to appoint a ***DPO***. The GDPR requires the following organisations to appoint a ***DPO***[16]:

- Public authorities or bodies;
- Organisations whose core activities involve regular, systematic and large-scale monitoring of data subjects; or
- Organisations core activities consist of the large-scale processing of ***Special Categories of Personal Data*** or data relating to criminal convictions and offences.

Therefore, the appointment of a ***DPO*** is applicable to maintained and academy schools who are a public authority. A public authority is

14 https://ico.org.uk/for-organisations/guide-to-data-protection/guide-to-the-general-data-protection-regulation-gdpr/children-and-the-gdpr/what-are-the-rules-about-an-iss-and-consent/

15 https://ico.org.uk/for-organisations/guide-to-data-protection/guide-to-the-general-data-protection-regulation-gdpr/consent/what-is-valid-consent/

16 Article 37 General Data Protection Regulation (EU) 2016/679

defined as a 'public authority defined under the Freedom of Information Act 2000'[17]. Therefore, if schools are subject to the Freedom of Information Act they will be legally obliged to appoint a ***DPO***. Even if not legally obliged to appoint a ***DPO*** (such as a private school), a school may wish to appoint one in any event.

Who Should it Be?

In terms of the appointment of a ***DPO***, the GDPR states that a ***DPO*** should be appointed on basis of their professional qualities and, in particular, their knowledge of data protection law and the ability to fulfil the specific roles and duties as a ***DPO*** as set out in the GDPR (for further details see 'The Role of the DPO' below).

We are often asked for advice as to who is best placed to fulfil the role of a ***DPO*** in a school and asked whether a senior member of staff can take on the appointment. There is nothing within the GDPR which prevents someone in a senior management position (e.g. a school business manager) from carrying out the role of ***DPO***. The GDPR allows ***DPOs*** to 'fulfil other tasks and duties' but requires that 'any such tasks and duties do not result in a conflict of interests[18]'. Guidance by the European Data Protection Board (a group of data protection officials from across the EU) suggests that individuals in senior management positions are likely to be conflicted[19]. However, the question of who can be a ***DPO*** will depend on the specific organisational structure of the school. There may be situations where the most appropriate person to take on the role is an individual in a senior management position, especially if they have existing compliance expertise. However, more practically we would recommend you assess who actually has the time to dedicate to the role, who has the authority to report directly to the highest level of management and who has the

17 Section 7(2) Data Protection Act 2018

18 Article 38(6) General Data Protection Regulation (EU) 2016/679

19 https://ec.europa.eu/newsroom/article29/item-detail.cfm?item_id=612048

expert data protection knowledge required to be a ***DPO*** by the GDPR[20].

In the case of a MAT, it is permissible to appoint a single ***DPO*** for all schools within the MAT as it is the MAT who has overall responsibility for the processing of personal data of the schools within it. However, the structure and size of the organisation must be taken into account. In practice, this means that it is feasible for a single ***DPO*** to look after data compliance across a whole MAT, however, if it is a particularly large MAT, one single ***DPO*** could be appointed and then have a support network working underneath them if necessary. In the case of a small school, they may have the opportunity to join together with a cluster of schools to share a ***DPO***. This could be done by way of a shared services agreement. Alternatively, you are able to outsource the role of ***DPO*** if you wish and have the resources to find it. There are third party organisations offering ***DPO*** services if you did not want to recruit for the role internally or externally.

The Role of the DPO

The GDPR sets out a list of tasks that a ***DPO*** is expected to conduct as a minimum. These are as follows[21]:

a) To inform and advise the school, and employees of the school, of their obligations under the GDPR and the DPA 2018;

b) To monitor the school's compliance with the GDPR, the DPA 2018 and any other applicable law, and with internal policies relating to data protection, including assigning responsibilities, awareness raising, staff training and data protection auditing;

c) To advise on data protection impact assessments and monitor the performance of assessments;

d) To co-operate with the ICO; and

---

20 Article 37(5) General Data Protection Regulation (EU) 2016/679

21 Article 39 General Data Protection Regulation (EU) 2016/679

e) To act as a contact point for the ICO on issues relating to processing of personal information.

In practice this is going to mean that the ***DPO*** will be responsible for ensuring the correct documentation is in place, organising staff data protection training, being the point of contact for data protection queries being raised in school, responding to subject access requests and liaising with ICO when necessary (e.g. in the event of a personal data breach).

Data Retention and the GDPR

The fifth Data Protection Principle states that personal information must not be kept for longer than is necessary[22]. This is a broad statement and the GDPR does not set any specific guidelines for how long personal information is to be kept. It is for individual organisations to decide how long to keep personal information for. It is unlikely that you will have a justification or legal basis for retaining personal information indefinitely and, from a practical point of view, schools are unlikely to have the resources to store large amounts of information.

In order to demonstrate compliance with this Data Protection Principle, the school should agree a retention policy or retention schedule which lists how long you will keep different types of personal information. The Department for Education's '*Data Protection: A Toolkit for Schools*[23]' provides extensive guidance for schools to consider when developing a data retention policy or schedule but is clear that it is for individual schools to set their own data retention schedules that are justifiable.

22 Article 5(1)(e) General Data Protection Regulation (EU) 2016/679

23 https://assets.publishing.service.gov.uk/government/uploads/system/uploads/attachment_data/file/747620/Data_Protection_Toolkit_for_Schools_OpenBeta.pdf

When setting data retention schedules, it is important that you do not focus solely on data protection issues. You will also need to consider your compliance with any other legal or regulatory requirements (e.g. you don't want to destroy a document in order to comply with the GDPR but end up committing a criminal offence as you've destroyed documents required by HMRC). Therefore, consider the following points when formalising a data retention schedule:

- Legal and regulatory compliance – Information relating to tax, health and safety and OFSTED requirements will have their own legal or regulatory retention periods; and
- Defence of legal claims – It is justifiable to keep personal information that would be required to defend legal proceedings for the relevant limitation period (i.e. the period of time in which the individual has to bring a claim).

There will be some information you do not need to keep at all once you know longer have a relationship with individual that has provided the information (e.g. emergency contacts for members of staff that have left).

Once you have agreed a data retention schedule, the periods of retention decided upon can be included within your record of processing (or Information Asset Register) to demonstrate your compliance with the GDPR.

CHAPTER THREE INDIVIDUALS' RIGHTS UNDER THE GDPR

One of the key aims of the GDPR is to empower individuals and give them control over their personal information. Individuals have a number of rights under the GDPR. These are:

1. **Right to be Forgotten**

This is a right introduced by the GDPR which enables an individual to request the deletion or removal of personal information where there is no compelling reason for its continued processing. This is not an absolute right. It will only apply in limited circumstances (e.g. where processing is based upon consent and the individual withdraws consent).

2. **Data Portability**

This is the right to get that personal data in a machine readable format. Individuals can also ask for their data to be transferred directly from one controller to another. There is no right to charge fees for this service.

3. **Right to Object to Direct Marketing**

The GDPR gives individuals the right to object to direct marketing. When an individual exercises this right, the organisation must not only stop sending direct marketing material to the individual, but also stop any processing of that individual's personal data for such marketing.

4. **Right to Rectification and Restriction**

The GDPR provides individuals with the right to have personal data rectified if it is inaccurate or incomplete. In addition, individuals also have the right to 'block' or suppress processing of personal data. When processing is restricted, you are permitted to store the personal data, but not further process it. You can retain just enough information about the individual to ensure that the restriction is respected in future.

5. **Subject Access Requests**

The GDPR gives individuals the right to be given a copy of their personal data from an organisation processing their personal data. This is discussed in more detail in the section "What is a SAR" below.

6. **Right to Complain**

The GDPR provides individuals with the the right to lodge a complaint with the ICO where their personal information has been processed in a way that does not comply with the GDPR. The GDPR obliges the ICO to investigate the complaint and inform the individual of the progress and the outcome of the investigation.

7. **Rights in relation to Profiling and Automated Decision Making**

Individuals have the right not to be subject to decisions made automatically that produce legal effects or significantly affect the individual. Individuals have the right to be notified about any profiling and may need to be given the opportunity to object to that profiling and somehow have some human intervention in the process.

Handling SARs from Pupils, Parents and Staff

As discussed above, under the GDPR individuals have a number of rights concerning their personal information. In this book we have focused on subject access requests as this is the most common request we see schools receiving.

What is a SAR?

Under the GDPR, an individual is entitled to be given a copy of their personal data from an organisation processing their personal data[1]. This is known as a subject access request or SAR. Along with a copy of their personal information, an individual is also entitled to receive information about:

- The reasons or purposes for which their personal data is being processed;
- The type of personal data concerned;
- Who that personal information has been shared with or disclosed to;
- How long their personal information will be held for;
- The source of the information;
- Information about how to make a complaint about how their personal information has been used; and
- If personal information has been transferred outside the European Economic Area, what safeguards are in place to protect their personal data.

In a school setting, a subject access request is most likely to come from a parent on behalf of their child (e.g. in the context of challenging a decision that has been made about their child) but it may also come

1 Article 15 General Data Protection Regulation (EU) 2016/679

from a pupil requesting access to their own information or from a member of staff (e.g. in the context of a grievance or disciplinary).

A SAR does not need to be in writing to be valid (e.g. by letter or e-mail). However, if a request is made by telephone or in person, the individual should be asked to put the request in writing so that the SAR is documented properly and the requester is properly identified but it is not a legal requirement. It may also be possible that a request is made in writing via text message or social media.

It can sometime be difficult to identify that a SAR is being made. The indication that a SAR is being made is that an individual will ask for all or any personal information that the school holds about them or their child. The request can be very broad (such as, 'give me a copy of all the information you hold about me') or it can be very precise ('give me a copy of the e-mail you sent about me yesterday'). A request does not need to include the words 'subject access request' or refer to the Data Protection Act or the GDPR. A request is valid even if the individual has not sent it directly to the person who normally deals with such requests. Therefore, it is important to ensure that all staff can recognise a subject access request and treat it appropriately.

How Long Do We Have to Respond?

SARs need to be responded to within 1 month of receipt[2]. This time period is set out in the GDPR and does not take into account school holidays. If a SAR is received during the school holidays it must still be responded to within a 1-month period.

In certain circumstances, you may be entitled to extend the period for responding by 2 months if the request is complex or a number of requests have been made. If you wish to extend the period for responding to the SAR, you must let the individual who made the request know within 1 month of receiving their request.

---

2 Article 12(3) General Data Protection Regulation (EU) 2016/679

Can we Charge a Fee?

In most cases you cannot charge a fee to respond to the SAR. However, there are certain circumstances where you may charge a reasonable fee which takes into account the administrative costs of providing the information or taking the action requested[3]. In these circumstances you must be able to show that the request is manifestly unfounded or excessive.

How to Approach a SAR?

You may have an internal procedure which sets out how you should handle a SAR and that should be referred to in the first instance. However, we suggest taking the following steps:

1. **SAR is received** – Whoever receives a SAR should forward it to their ***Data Protection Officer*** or other nominated person. You will need to make a note of the date it was received and calculate the date your response is due in 1 months' time.

2. **Checking identity or authority to make SAR** – If a parent makes a SAR on behalf of their child, you will need to consider the age of the child before any information is disclosed to the parent. Once a pupil is old enough to be able to understand their rights over their own information (generally considered to be age 12 but this will depend on each individual child), you will need to get permission from the pupil to disclose their information to their parent.

   In some cases, it may be appropriate to verify the identity of the individual making the SAR. It is important that you do not send copies of personal information to people where you are not sure of their identity but you should not appear obstructive. If you are unsure of a person's identity you should take reasonable

3 Article 12(5) General Data Protection Regulation (EU) 2016/679

measures to verify their identity (e.g. photo ID and proof of address). You should keep a record of what measures you take to verify their identity. Where there is no doubt about the person's identity (e.g. they are a member of staff or a parent who has had regular contact with the school) then it is unlikely you would need to verify their identity.

3. **Clarify the request if necessary** – If the SAR is unclear or is very broad, contact the person making the SAR to seek clarification or to provide further detail to enable you to locate the information they have asked for. You may wish to request further information regarding the context of the information or dates when it was processed. This could be done by asking the individual to complete a standardised SAR form if you have one.

4. **Retrieval of information** – You will need to decide where personal information about the individual might be held and locate that information. If the SAR relates to a pupil this may include:

    - Pupil files;
    - SEN files, reviews and education plans;
    - Child protection files;
    - Complaints files;
    - Accident book;
    - Correspondence including letters and e-mails relating to the pupil.

    You may need to speak to a number of different members of staff who might hold information about the pupil in different areas.

    If the SAR relates to a member of staff, this may include searching:

- Personnel files;
- Complaints file;
- Accident book;
- Correspondence including letters and e-mails relating to the member of staff.

In any type of SAR, you should ensure that you undertake a search of all relevant email accounts, your computer system, relevant paper records and any files and network folders. If relevant, you will also need to check CCTV records.

5. **Review the information** – Once you have conducted your search and collated the information held about the individual, you must examine it in detail to establish if it can be disclosed to the person making the SAR. To do this you will need to examine each document that has been retrieved as part of your search. In some cases, you might have to disclose only a part of the of particular document. You will also need to make sure that the information is actually about the person concerned and not someone else with the same name and screen out any duplicate records.

<u>Third Party Information</u>

You should take care to only disclose information about the person making the request. If a document contains personal information about other people, you should not disclose that document unless you have the consent of the other people named in the document to disclose it. If you cannot get consent from the other people named in the document, you must consider whether it is reasonable to disclose the information or redact the information about other people so that they cannot be identified.

Prevention or detection of crime

You must not disclose information which would prejudice the prevention or detection of a crime[4]. For example, if the police informed the school that a pupil is under investigation but the individual concerned was not aware of this, then you should not provide any information related to the investigation to the pupil or their family whilst the investigation is in progress. However, if the investigation is closed, or if the pupil has been informed that there is an investigation underway, then some or all of the information could be disclosed in response to a SAR.

Legal privilege

You must not disclose any records which contain advice from your legal representatives or where you are asking for legal advice or which were written as part of obtaining legal advice[5]. For example, if the school has asked its solicitors for legal advice to assist in a dismissal of a member of staff, that correspondence must not be provided to the member of staff if they make a SAR.

Other exemptions

In addition to the exemptions listed above, the DPA 2018 contains a number of other exemptions. These include personal information which is processed for management forecasting or planning, information which records negotiations with the data subject and confidential references[6].

---

4 Schedule 2 Part 1(2) Data Protection Act 2018

5 Schedule 2 Part 4(19) Data Protection Act 2018

6 Schedule 2 Part 4 Data Protection Act 2018

Destruction of information

You must not destroy information because it would be embarrassing to disclose. This is a criminal offence if it is done after a SAR has been made[7]. As you conduct your search for information, you may find documents which may damage the reputation of the school or members of staff. For example, you may find documents which show that standard procedures were not followed, or comments in e-mails which will cause offence to the individual. These documents must be disclosed unless there is an exemption which applies to them.

Redaction

If you have to redact information (e.g. to remove third party information), you should print off a copy of the document, then make the redactions using a black permanent marker pen ensuring that the entirety of the relevant information is covered. You may need to photocopy the information and mark the redactions again using black permanent marker pen. You need to be satisfied that the redacted information is not legible. The ICO provides further guidance on redacting information and this can be found on the ICO website[8].

6. **Responding to the SAR** – Your response to the SAR must be in writing. If the request was made via e-mail, then you should respond in the same way unless otherwise agreed with the individual making the request. You will need to prepare a response letter setting out all of the information discussed in the section **"What is a SAR?"** above. The majority of this information will already been provided in the relevant privacy notice (e.g. if a parent is making a request on behalf of their child, look at your privacy notice for parents or if it is a member of staff, look at

7 Section 173 Data Protection Act 2018

8 https://ico.org.uk/media/2013958/how-to-disclose-information-safely.pdf

your privacy notice for your workforce) so consulting the privacy notice will provide you with the majority of the information you need to provide in your response. You will also need to provide a copy of the information you have reviewed and redacted where necessary.

Can a SAR be made on someone else's behalf?

There may be circumstances where someone else makes a SAR on behalf of an individual. For example, this could be a parent making a SAR on behalf of their child or a solicitor acting on behalf of a member of staff. In these cases, you need to be satisfied that the third party making the request is entitled to act on behalf of the individual.

In the case of parent making a SAR on behalf of their child, you will need to consider the age of the child before any information is disclosed to the parent. Once a pupil is old enough to be able to understand their rights over their own information (generally considered to be age 12 but this will depend on each individual child), you will need to get permission from the pupil to disclose their information to their parent (e.g. a signed letter stating that the pupil gives their parent permission to make the SAR on their behalf).

In the case of a solicitor making a SAR on their client's behalf, this should be a signed written authority to make the request.

What are the consequences of not handling a SAR properly?

There may be serious consequences for the school for failing to comply with a SAR properly. These include:

- A complaint being made to the ICO – Individuals may complain to the ICO about how the SAR has been handled. This could result in an investigation by the ICO where they serve an enforcement notice ordering you to comply with the SAR correctly or even a fine for not complying with data protection laws;

- Court order for disclosure – Individuals have the ability to seek a court order requiring you to disclose information[9]; and
- Compensation – Individuals may have the right to compensation if they suffer distress or damage as a result of your failure to comply with data protection laws[10].

Requests for Pupil Educational Records

In addition to rights under the data protection laws, parents of children at maintained schools have an independent right of access to their child's educational record under the Education (Pupil Information) (England) Regulations 2005 or, for pupils in Wales, the Pupil Information (Wales) Regulations 2011.

What is an educational record?

A pupil's educational record is any record of information which:

- Is processed by or on behalf of the governing body of, or a teacher at, any school maintained by a local authority or any special school which is not maintained;
- Relates to a pupil or former pupil at the school;
- Originates or was supplied by any employee of the local authority who maintains the school, a teacher or other employee of a special school, the pupil in question and the parents of that pupil[11].

---

9 Section 167 Data Protection Act 2018

10 Sections 168 and 169 Data Protection Act 2018

11 Regulation 3 Education (Pupil Information) (England) Regulations 2005

Therefore, an educational record will commonly include information such as records of academic achievements, education, health and care plans and personal education plans. It will also include any correspondence from teachers, local education authority employees and educational psychologists engaged by the school. It may also include information from the pupil and the parent.

Who has a right of access to an educational record?

The right of access of a pupil's educational record is available to a parent (defined by s.576 of the Education Act 1996) and includes any person who has parental responsibility for the child or who has care of them[12].

How long do we have to respond to a request access to an educational record?

You must make the educational record available for inspection or provide a copy of the record to the parent making the request within 15 school days of the written request.

Can we charge a fee for responding to the request?

You cannot charge to make a record available to a parent for inspection but you can make a small administrative charge for copying the educational record. Any charge must be set by your governing body and must not exceed your cost of supplying the copy of the educational record[13].

When can a request to see an educational record be refused?

The right of access to the educational record is a right granted to parents of maintained schools and a pupil cannot refuse the right to their parents. However, there are certain circumstances where the school can

12 Regulation 5 Education (Pupil Information) (England) Regulations 2005

13 Regulation 5 Education (Pupil Information) (England) Regulations 2005

withhold an educational record (e.g. where the information might cause serious harm to the physical or mental health of the pupil or another individual). You can also deny the request if it would mean releasing examination marks before they are officially announced[14].

Does the right of access to educational records apply to academies or independent schools?

The right of access to the educational record is a right granted to parents of maintained schools only and there is no equivalent legal right of access to parents of academies, free schools, independent schools or colleges.

What is the difference between a SAR and request to see the educational record?

There are a number of differences between a SAR and a request to see an educational record including:

- The right to access an educational record only applies to maintained schools and special schools whereas all pupils have the right to make a SAR;
- The right to access an educational record only applies to very specific information whereas a SAR applies to all personal information;
- The right to access an educational record is the parents' rights whereas the right to make a SAR is the pupil's right which a parent can exercise on the pupil's behalf;
- The time limit for responding to a request to access an educational record is shorter but takes into account school days whereas the time limit to respond to an SAR is more general and does not take into account term times; and

---

14 Regulation 5 Education (Pupil Information) (England) Regulations 2005

- There are a wide range of exemptions available under data protection laws.

As there is some overlap between the different requests, it may be necessary to clarify with the person making the request what type of information they require and what type of request they want to make.

Case Study

An Academy receives an e-mail from a non-resident father whose son is a Year 10 pupil at the school. The school is aware that the pupil has not seen his father for a number of years. The e-mail states that the father wants "*a copy of all the information you have about my son's attendance, achievements and wellbeing.*" The e-mail explains that the father wants this information as he is taking court action for access to his son. The e-mail does not refer to the Education (Pupil Information) (England) Regulations 2005, the DPA or the GDPR.

The e-mail could be construed as either a request for a copy of an education record or a SAR. The school writes back to the father to inform him that he cannot make a request for a copy of his son's educational record as that right only applies to parents of pupils of maintained schools and it is not applicable to academies. The school informs him that he could make a subject access request on behalf of his child but, given that his son is 14, he would need to obtain his son's permission to make the request on his behalf. The father is unable to get this permission from his son so the school is unable to respond to the SAR.

What about FOI Requests?

The Freedom of Information Act 2000 (FOIA) applies to schools that are defined as 'public authorities'. In the case of academies this is restricted to "academy business". The FOIA permits the public access to information held by a public authority (e.g. details of expenses claimed by senior management teams over a period of time or details of how many pupils have been excluded over a period of time). There are a number of exemptions to the right of access under the FOIA. In particular, information does not have to be disclosed under the FOIA if doing so would breach the school's obligations to protection personal information under the GDPR.

Detailed analysis of FOIA falls outside the scope of this book.

CHAPTER FOUR
INFORMATION SHARING

When and How?

By 'information sharing' we mean the disclosure of personal data from one organisation to another. In this chapter we will focus on the sharing of personal data between a school and other ***Data Controllers*** (such as other schools and colleges, local authorities and OFSTED). In the next chapter (Data Processors) we will focus on sharing information with ***Data Processors*** (such as third-party suppliers like outsourced IT providers or payroll services). The GDPR makes a distinction between a ***Data Controller*** and a ***Data Processor*** and there are a number of steps to take when employing the services of a ***Data Processor*** which are discussed in detail at chapter 5.

Common examples of information sharing with Data Controllers:

- Local authority;
- OFSTED;
- DfE;
- Pension providers;
- Trade Unions;
- Solicitors;
- Accountants;
- Exam boards.

When can we share information with other Data Controllers?

In order for any information sharing to be compliant with the GDPR, it must be done lawfully, fairly and in a transparent manner so that it complies with the first Data Protection Principle. It is vital to point out at the outset that data protection is not a barrier to sharing information when there is a risk to a pupil's health or safety (see below **'Keeping Children Safe'** for further details).

Article 6 of the GDPR sets out 6 different ways in which information sharing can be justified. The sharing of personal data will be lawful if at least one of the following applies:

(a) The individual has given you their consent to do so;

(b) It is necessary for the performance of a contract or to enter into a contract with the individual;

(c) It is necessary for compliance with a legal obligation;

(d) It is necessary in order to protect the vital interests of an individual;

(e) It is necessary for the performance of a task carried out in the public interest or in the exercise of official authority vested in the controller; or

(f) It is necessary for the purposes of the legitimate interests of the controller.

If you wish to share more sensitive ***Special Category Personal Data*** (such as information relating to health, disabilities or sexuality), you must also ensure that one of the following conditions set out in Article 9 of the GDPR apply (in addition to the conditions listed above):

(a) You have obtained explicit consent from the individual;

(b) It is necessary in order for the school to carry out its obligations under employment, social security or social protection law;

(c) It is necessary to protect the vital interests of an individual;

(d) The information has already been manifestly made public by the individual concerned;

(e) It is necessary for the conducting or defending legal claims;

(f) It is necessary for reasons of substantial public interest (as set out in the DPA 2018[1]);

(g) It is necessary for assessing the working capacity of an employee;

(h) It is necessary for archiving purposes in the public interest.

These conditions are discussed in further detail below.

Legal Obligation

Where information is being shared by a school to another ***Data Controller***, it is most likely being shared because you are legally obliged to share the information or it is necessary to safely and effectively run the school.

If you are legally obliged to share information (e.g. DfE data returns such as the school census), your legal basis to share information is set out in Article 6 of the GDPR (compliance with a legal obligation)[2]. If your legal obligation to share information includes ***Special Category Personal Data*** (e.g. information relating to equality and diversity), then your legal basis' for sharing that information under the GDPR is set out in Article 6 (compliance with a legal obligation) and Article 9 (necessary for reasons of substantial public interest[3]).

---

1 Schedule 1 Part 2 Data Protection Act 2018

2 Article 6(1)(c) General Data Protection Regulation (EU) 2016/679

3 Article 9(2)(g) General Data Protection Regulation (EU) 2016/679

Public Interest

If you share personal information with another ***Data Controller***, but you do not have a legal obligation to do so, you may have another lawful basis under the GDPR if the sharing of information is necessary to safely and effectively run the school (e.g. in order for you to provide education or carry out school improvements). In these circumstances, you may have a lawful basis for sharing that information under Article 6 of the GDPR (necessary for the performance of a task in the public interest)[4].

If you are relying on the 'public interest' legal basis in the GDPR for sharing information and that information contains ***Special Category Personal Data***, you will also need to identify an appropriate legal basis in Article 9 of the GDPR (see '**When can we share information with other Data Controllers?**' above).

Performance of a Contract

It is likely that you are required to share information about your workforce with other ***Data Controllers*** in order to fulfill your duties as an employer (e.g. sharing information with pension providers or your insurers). In these circumstances, your legal basis to share personal information about your workforce is likely to be Article 6 of the GDPR (necessary to perform a contract).

If you are relying on the 'necessary to perform a contract' legal basis in the GDPR for sharing information and that information contains ***Special Category Personal Data***, you will also need to identify an appropriate legal basis in Article 9 of the GDPR (see '**When can we share information with other Data Controllers?**' above).

---

4 Article 6(1)(e) General Data Protection Regulation (EU) 2016/679

Consent

If you are not under a legal obligation to share the information or it is not necessary to run the school safely and effectively, you may need consent to share that information. In a school setting, consent is the least likely legal basis for processing personal information and should only be considered where none of the other conditions apply. In a school setting, consent is most likely to be required for the following types of information sharing:

- To share photographs of pupils online, in marketing material and/or in the local press; or
- To make voluntary referrals to external organisations (e.g. to sign a pupil up to external music or foreign language lessons); or
- Circulating lists of names and/or addresses to allow for pupils to send each other greeting cards.

If consent is required, the school will need to consider the practical implications this brings such as ensuring the consent is obtained from the correct person (i.e. the pupil or their parent/guardian), the consent is valid and you are able to facilitate the withdrawal of consent if needed (see Chapter 2 'School's Obligations under the GDPR' for further information).

Use of Information Sharing Agreements

Where you regularly share personal information with another ***Data Controller*** (e.g. your local authority), it is recommended that you have an information sharing agreement in place[5]. This will set out clearly what personal information is being shared, justify the sharing of

5 https://ico.org.uk/media/for-organisations/documents/1068/data_sharing_code_of_practice.pdf

personal information and will help demonstrate the school's compliance with the GDPR.

There is no specific form of data sharing agreement (unlike with a data processing agreement as discussed at Chapter 5). However, the ICO Data Sharing Code of Practice advises that the following questions should be dealt with in an information sharing agreement:

- What is the purpose of the information sharing (e.g. to ensure young people don't go missing in education, to monitor pupil attendance, to ensure schools and pupils are properly supported)?
- Which other organisations will be involved?
- What personal information is going to be shared (e.g. pupil details, attendance details, exclusions details, free school meals eligibility etc.)?
- Is there any ***Special Category Personal Data*** (e.g. details of special educational needs)?
- What is your lawful basis for sharing (e.g. in order to comply with a legal obligation, performance of a task in the public interest)?
- How will you share information (e.g. by secure data encryption)?
- What governance arrangements need to be in place (e.g. how should breaches be dealt with, how will requests by individuals be handled, how should information be disposed of etc.)?

Once information sharing agreements are developed, any staff involved in the sharing of personal information will need to be made aware of the contents of the agreement and training provided where necessary (e.g. to ensure any technical and security arrangements are complied with). Any information sharing agreements should then be reviewed regularly (e.g. annually) to ensure the arrangements set out in the agreement are still adequate and work in practice.

Keeping Children Safe

Data protection should not be a barrier to information sharing and there is nothing in the GDPR or the DPA 2018 which limits the sharing of information for the purposes of keeping children and young people safe. All staff should receive appropriate safeguarding and child protection training and any concerns regarding safeguarding should be dealt with in accordance with your safeguarding/child protection policy and raised with the school's designated safeguarding lead[6].

The GDPR and the DPA 2018 permit the sharing of ***Special Category Personal Data*** without consent where it is to keep a child or young personal safe from neglect or physical, emotional or mental harm, or if it is to protect their physical, mental or emotional well-being[7].

Whilst there is a lawful basis in the GDPR to share information to keep pupils safe, you also need to make sure you comply with the remainder of the data protection principles when making a disclosure. Therefore, your considerations are more like to centre on how to make a disclosure rather than whether or not to actually make the disclosure in the first place. If you decide you need to make a disclosure in order to keep a pupil safe, you must also make sure the information shared is:

- Necessary and proportionate – The information you disclose must be proportionate to the need and level of risk;
- Relevant – only share the information which is relevant to the disclosure you are making;

---

6 Keeping Children Safe in Education 2019

7 Schedule 1 Part 2 (18) Data Protection Act 2018

- Accurate – Information disclosed should be accurate and up to date;
- Timely – If you feel a disclosure needs to be made, it should be done in a timely manner to reduce the risk of harm to a pupil; and
- Secure – Information disclosed needs to be shared securely (e.g. so that it is only accessed by people authorised to see it).

Where there are circumstances in which you are required to make a disclosure in order to keep a pupil safe, that decision should be recorded[8]. You should document the reasons why you have decided to make a decision and record exactly what information was given and to whom it was disclosed to. This will ensure that, in the event of any complaint being made, the school is able to demonstrate its reasons for making the disclosure as well as being able to confirm what was disclosed.

Case Study

A school has joined a multi-agency panel to discuss children and young people with additional needs who would benefit from a multi-agency input. The panel has representatives from education, health, social-care, youth justice and youth work staff. Representatives from the panel have all entered into a Service Level Agreement (SLA) but the SLA does not cover specific details relating to information sharing. Ahead of the next panel meeting, the school has been asked to provide a behaviour and education update in relation to one of the pupils the panel is supporting. The schools' representative sent the update back to the panel members but accidentally copied in an individual from another organisation in error.

The panel decided to review how it shared information as a result of the error and decided to enter into an information sharing agreement. Part

8 Information Sharing: Advice for Practitioners providing Safeguarding Services to Children, Young People. Parents and Carers July 2018

of the information sharing agreement explicitly stated that any information shared must be sent by encrypted e-mail or be password protected. This would reduce the risk of harm to the young people the panel were supporting if such an error occurred again.

CHAPTER FIVE
DATA PROCESSORS

Who is a Data Processor?

As discussed earlier, the school is a '*Data Controller*' as it is the organisation who decides the manner and purpose of how personal data is collected and used. In contrast, a '*Data Processor*' is an organisation or individual that processes personal information on behalf of a *Data Controller* – so the school decides whether or not to provide the *Data Processor* with personal information in the first place, what personal information to send and gives the *Data Processor* instructions as to what to do with the personal information. A *Data Processor* is not an employee of the *Data Controller*. Practically speaking, a *Data Processor* is a third-party supplier with access to personal information.

In a school setting, common examples of *Data Processors* are:

- Caterers and cleaners;
- Outsourced payroll providers;
- Outsourced HR providers;
- IT providers;
- Teaching and learning portals;
- Organisations providing you with reports and analysis of your exam results;
- Confidential waste disposal;
- Off-site data storage including cloud based services.

What is the difference between a Data Controller and a Data Processor?

The GDPR makes a distinction between ***Data Controllers*** and ***Data Processors*** and there are a number of factors to consider when employing the services of a ***Data Processor*** (discussed further in the section 'What is Required' below). Therefore, it is important to consider whether your third-party suppliers or partners are ***Data Processors*** or ***Data Controllers*** in their own right.

The key difference between a ***Data Controller*** and a ***Data Processor*** is the level of independence each party has in using personal data. ***Data Processors*** only use the information they are given under the instructions of the ***Data Controller***. Guidance produced by the European Data Protection Board[1] says you should look at the following factors to consider whether a third party is a ***Data Controller*** or a ***Data Processor***:

- The level of instructions given to the party processing personal information which determines the degree of independence a ***Data Processor*** can exercise;
- The monitoring by the ***Data Controller*** of the execution of the service; and
- The expertise of the parties – in some cases, the role and professional expertise of a service provider will play a predominant role, which may result in the third party being a ***Data Controller*** in its own right.

In a school setting, common examples of other ***Data Controllers*** are:

- Local authority;
- OFSTED;

1 https://ec.europa.eu/justice/article-29/documentation/opinion-recommendation/files/2010/wp169_en.pdf

- DfE;
- Pension providers;
- Trade Unions;
- Solicitors;
- Accountants;
- Exam boards;
- Police;
- NHS.

What is required?

The school is responsible for ensuring ***Data Processors*** comply with the GDPR. Therefore if the school engages a ***Data Processor*** who does not comply with the GDPR, the school could face enforcement action and potential fines from the ICO and potential claims for compensation from affected individuals.

The GDPR places an obligation on the school, as a ***Data Controller***, to only use ***Data Processors*** who can provide you with sufficient guarantees that they have appropriate technical and organisational security measures in place that meet the requirements set out in the GDPR[2].

In addition, the school is required to have a written contract with all its ***Data Processors*** which fulfils certain requirements set out in the GDPR. The GDPR is very specific about what the contract must include[3]. In particular, the contract with the ***Data Processor*** must confirm that the ***Data Processor*** will:

2 Article 28(1) General Data Protection Regulation (EU) 2016/679

3 Article 28(3) General Data Protection Regulation (EU) 2016/679

- Only process personal information on documented instructions of the school;
- Ensure that persons authorised to process the personal information (e.g. employees of the ***Data Processor***) are subject to a duty of confidentiality (e.g. in their employment contract);
- Take all necessary security measures as required by the GDPR;
- Not engage another ***Data Processor*** (e.g. a sub-contractor) without the written authorisation of the school;
- Assist the school in fulfilling any of your obligations, as ***Data Controller***, if an individual makes a subject access request (or another request under the GDPR);
- Assist the school in fulfilling your obligations to take all necessary security measures, notify you of any ***Personal Data Breach*** and assist you in conducting a Data Protection Impact Assessment (DPIA) where applicable;
- Delete or return personal information to you at the end of the provision of services; and
- Make available to the school all information necessary to demonstrate compliance with the GDPR, including allowing for audits and inspections conducted by the school or an auditor on the school's behalf.

This written contract could form part of your supplier's standard terms and conditions or could be through a standalone data processing agreement.

Practical Steps to Take

Given that the school is responsible for ensuring ***Data Processors*** comply with the GDPR, we have made some practical suggestions below of steps to take to ensure you comply with GDPR.

Existing Third-Party Suppliers

Where you have existing contracts with suppliers in place, we suggest taking the following steps:

1. Make a list of all your existing third-party suppliers who are ***Data Processors***;
2. Review the terms of the contract with your suppliers to see whether the contracts contain clauses which cover all those listed in the section 'What is Required?' above;
3. Send suppliers a GDPR questionnaire to complete so that the school can assess the supplier's level of GDPR compliance; and
4. If the terms of the contract do not include the necessary GDPR clauses, request that the supplier sends you a data processing agreement for you to sign.

New Third-Party Suppliers

Where you want to engage a new third-party supplier, we suggest taking the following steps:

1. Ask the supplier to complete a GDPR questionnaire so that the school can assess the supplier's level of GDPR compliance;
2. Review the terms of the proposed contract sent by the supplier to see whether the contract contains clauses which cover all those listed in the section 'What is Required?' above;

3. If the proposed contract does not contain the necessary clauses, ask the supplier to amend the contract so that it complies with the GDPR.

Once you have assessed the level of GDPR compliance the ***Data Processor*** has and have ensured the correct contract terms are in place, your responsibility as a ***Data Controller*** does not end there. You should have procedures in place to review your ***Data Processor's*** compliance on an ongoing basis (e.g. annually or at the time of renewal of the contract) in order for to you to be able to demonstrate your own compliance with the GDPR and, in particular, the '***accountability principle***'.

CHAPTER SIX
EMAILS, WEBSITES AND SOCIAL MEDIA

There is no doubt that the internet can be a useful resource but one that has to be carefully managed in order to reduce risk to safety, wellbeing and reputation. Data protection concerns are just one of many concerns schools face by the use of e-mails, websites and social media. Keeping Children Safe in Education 2019, the statutory guidance on safeguarding children, is clear that there should be a whole school approach to online safety[1]. Ensuring compliance with the GDPR and the DPA 2018 will play a part in this whole school approach.

E-mails

The use of e-mail is now commonplace in most schools but the use of e-mail can pose a risk to schools' data protection compliance. E-mails are often described as a 'plain text postcard' that could potentially be read by any of the servers they pass through or from unauthorised users who have hacked into a system. Many schools may have, or be in the process of developing, a secure e-mail system which means that all e-mails are encrypted by default and that only the intended recipients of the e-mail will be able to access it.

However, the more likely problem is e-mails being sent to the wrong recipient. The use of e-mail and e-mails being sent to the incorrect recipient are one of the most commonly reported ***Personal Data Breaches***[2]. This can be particularly problematic if the e-mail contains ***Special Category Personal Data*** or includes an attachment which was confidential (e.g. contained an SEN report).

---

1 Keeping Children Safe in Education 2019

2 https://ico.org.uk/action-weve-taken/data-security-incident-trends/

The risk of such ***Personal Data Breaches*** can be reduced if security measures are put in place to reduce this risk. For example, you should password protect documents containing ***Special Category Personal Data*** so that even if the e-mail is sent to the wrong recipient, the attachment cannot be opened. In addition, it may be possible to put a delay on your outgoing e-mails so that if you realise shortly after sending that the e-mail was sent to the wrong recipient, you can recover the e-mail from your Outbox. It may also be possible to disable certain features in your e-mail system such as the 'Reply All' feature or 'Auto Complete' which would reduce the risk of e-mails being sent to the wrong recipient in error.

Example

Stoke-on-Trent City Council were fined £120,000 in October 2012 (under the previous Data Protection Act 1998) after a ***Personal Data Breach*** that involved a misdirected e-mail[3]. A solicitor for the Council sent a number of e-mails to a wrong e-mail address by mistake. The e-mails varied in sensitivity but some contained confidential and highly sensitive (now known as ***Special Category***) information about a child protection case. The e-mails were not sent via the Council's secure e-mail system or encrypted when they could have been. The investigation by the ICO found that there was a lack of appropriate data protection training and this contributed towards the level of fine the ICO imposed.

Websites

School's IT filtering and monitoring systems not only work to reduce the risk of pupils being exposed to illegal, inappropriate or harmful material, but they also play an important part of your GDPR compliance. Securing the school's IT system will help ensure that all the personal data stored on it is kept safe and cannot be accessed by unauthorised

---

3 https://www.bbc.co.uk/news/uk-england-stoke-staffordshire-20083120

users. Any IT security measures that you have will form part of the technical and organisational measures the school puts in place to demonstrate compliance with the ***'integrity and confidentiality principle'***.

You should also be mindful of the information you publish on the school's own website. If the website displays pupil's personal information (e.g. photographs or academic achievements), it has the potential to be viewed by anyone and needs to be treated differently to information that is only displayed within the school. Prior to publishing personal information on the school's website, you will need to consider what your lawful basis is to process pupil information in that way. In this circumstance, consent will be the appropriate legal basis to process personal information (Article 6(1)(a) GDPR) and the consent to publish the information online will need to be obtained from either the parent or carer or the pupil, depending on their age. For further information in relation to consent, please see Chapter 2 ('**The Question of Consent**').

Social Media

In most circumstances, the use of social media by individuals is not subject to the GDPR or the Data Protection Act 2018. The GDPR does not apply to personal information used in the course of purely personal or household activity. We are often asked by schools whether or not a parent 'naming and shaming' a teacher online is a breach of data protection legislation. The short answer is 'no' as the parent is not subject to the GDPR or the Data Protection Act 2018 and the ICO will not intervene with parents' use of social media. In these situations, we would advise to report any abusive comments on social media to the social media company in question and, if necessary, report harassment or malicious communications to the police.

Whilst an individual's use of social media is not subject to the GDPR, the schools' use of social media will be. Therefore when publishing personal information on social media, the school must make sure it complies with all the data protection principles. This includes having a lawful basis under the GDPR to process the personal information in this way. If the school wanted to publish personal information on a social media account (e.g. a photograph of pupils on a school trip), consent is the appropriate lawful basis to do this under the GDPR (Article 6(1)(a)) and the consent to publish the information online will need to be obtained from either the parent or carer or the pupil, depending on their age. For further information in relation to consent, please see Chapter 2 ('**The Question of Consent**').

CHAPTER SEVEN
BREACHES – PREVENTION AND MITIGATION

Prevention – Suggested Security Measures, Policies and Procedures

The saying "*prevention is better than a cure*" is certainly true in a world of data protection. ***Personal Data Breaches*** not only cause you problems with the ICO but can result in claims for compensation and adverse publicity, not to mention the amount of time it takes for a number of staff to investigate a breach and deal with the subsequent fall out.

As discussed earlier, one of the data protection principles is to process personal information securely and take both technical and organisational measures to protect against unauthorised processing, loss destruction or damage of personal data[1].

Organisational Measures – Policies and Procedures

Building a culture of data protection in your school is the best form of prevention. This can be done through a variety of organisational measures. The starting point is your policies and procedures. An overarching data protection policy will set out how the school proposes to comply with the GDPR. In addition, you should also have the following documented policies and procedures:

- Data breach procedure;
- Acceptable ICT use policy;
- Data retention policy;
- Bring your own device policy;

1 Article 5 General Data Protection Regulation (EU) 2016/679

- Use of CCTV;
- Child protection and safeguarding policy;
- Subject access procedure.

You may already take a number of steps to protect personal data (e.g. keeping paper records under lock and key when not being used) which you could document in your data protection policy to demonstrate the school's compliance with the GDPR. These may include:

- Locking computer screens when people are away from their desks;
- Tidy desks so that no paper documents containing personal data are left unattended on desks;
- Ensuring all paper documents are disposed of confidentially;
- Prohibiting members of staff sending work to personal e-mail accounts as they are not secure and risk being hacked.

In the event of having to report a ***Personal Data Breach*** to the ICO (see below section '**When to Notify the ICO**') or a complaint being made about you, one of the questions you will be asked by the ICO is what policies and procedures you have in place. It is important to be able to point towards your documented policies and procedures and demonstrate that staff are aware of their contents.

Organisational Measures – Training

A data protection culture can also be built by regular training of staff. In order to ensure the school's compliance with the GDPR, staff need to understand the importance of data protection and be familiar with your data protection policies and procedures.

Training should be provided on induction and then at regular intervals (e.g. at least once a year). This training should include:

- The school's responsibilities as a ***Data Controller***;
- Staff's responsibilities for protecting personal data and the risks of failing to do so;
- The proper procedures to identify callers;
- Disclosing personal data to third parties;
- Recognising a subject access request; and
- Procedure to follow in the event of a ***Personal Data Breach***.

A key part of this training will be highlighting the importance of staff reporting breaches or suspected breaches of the GDPR to the DPO (or other relevant member of staff) immediately. This will ensure that the school is made aware of the breach and can deal with the breach in a timely manner. Having a standardised Personal Data Breach report which staff can fill out in the event of a breach will be useful in order for you to quickly gather the relevant information. A template ***Personal Data Breach*** Report Form can be found at Appendix B.

In the event of having to report a ***Personal Data Breach*** to the ICO (see below section '**When to Notify the ICO**') or a complaint being made about you, one of the questions you will be asked by the ICO when did members of staff last receive data protection training and what did the training entail. It is important to be able to document what training staff have been given and when it was last completed.

Technical measures

There are a wide range of technical security measures which the school can put in place to prevent ***Personal Data Breaches***. The GDPR does not set specific security standards. Instead, it takes a risk-based approach to ensure a level of security appropriate to the risk that a loss of personal information would pose. These measures may include:

- Encryption;

- Being able to ensure ongoing confidentiality, integrity, availability and resilience of systems and services processing personal information;
- Ability to restore availability and access to personal information quickly in the event of a technical incident; and
- Processes for regularly testing and evaluating the effectiveness of your technical and organisational security measures.

In a school setting, common examples of technical measures to help prevent ***Personal Data Breaches*** include:

- Password protecting attachments to e-mails containing confidential or ***Special Category Personal Data***;
- Setting a delay on sending e-mails in Outlook so that e-mails sent in error can be retrieved;
- Prohibiting the use of removable media (e.g. USBs, smartphones, tablets) without authorisation from your ICT team;
- Prohibiting access to personal e-mail accounts from the school network;

Breach Damage Limitation

In the event of a ***Personal Data Breach***, your investigation will want to establish whether or not the breach is still occurring. If so, steps must be taken immediately to minimise the impact and effect of the breach.

Your ***DPO***, or other nominated person, will need to quickly take any necessary steps to recover any losses and limit the damage caused by the ***Personal Data Breach***. These steps may include:

- Attempting to recover lost equipment or documents;

- In the event of a 'phishing' attack, contact all members of staff to warn them of the nature of the phishing e-mail that was sent;
- Advising staff to immediately change passwords or entry codes if the breach involved access via passwords or entry codes; and
- Consider whether the Police need to be informed where you believe a criminal offence may have been committed.

Your data breach procedure should include details of what steps to take to attempt to reduce the effect of the ***Personal Data Breach***. In the event of a breach which is reportable to the ICO or is reported to the ICO by an individual making a complaint, the ICO will want to know what steps you have taken to contain the breach. If you are able to demonstrate you acted quickly and took steps to contain the breach promptly, this will be a mitigating factor that the ICO will take into account when deciding whether any enforcement action is necessary.

When to Notify the ICO

One of the main changes introduced by the GDPR was the requirement for ***Personal Data Breaches*** to be reported to the ICO within 72 hours in certain circumstances[2]. There is also a duty to communicate the breach to individuals in certain circumstances.

The obligation to report ***Personal Data Breaches*** is set out in Article 33 of the GDPR:

> *"In the case of a personal data breach, the controller shall without undue delay and, where feasible, no later than 72 hours after having become aware of it, notify the personal data breach to the Supervisory Authority... unless the personal data breach is unlikely to result in a risk to the rights freedoms of natural persons".*

---

2 Article 33 General Data Protection Regulation (EU) 2016/679

Has there been a "Personal Data Breach"?

The first point to consider when there has been an incident, is to determine whether or not there has actually been a ***Personal Data Breach.*** Not all breaches of the GDPR amount to a ***Personal Data Breach.*** If the incident does not meet the definition of a ***Personal Data Breach*** as set out in the GDPR, it is not notifiable to the ICO.

The GDPR defines personal data breach in Article 4(12) as:

> *"A breach of security leading to the accidental or unlawful destruction, loss, alteration, unauthorised disclosure of, or access to, personal data transmitted, stored or otherwise processed".*

Most commonly, it will be instances where information has been disclosed to the incorrect person or has been accessed by someone who is not supposed to see the information that is going to cause you concern. However, it should also be noted that other instances can amount to a ***Personal Data Breach*** such as where information has been altered, corrupted or is no longer available. In that regard, ***Personal Data Breaches*** can be categorised according to three well known information security principles:

1. A confidentiality breach – this is where there is an unauthorised or accidental disclosure of or access to personal data.

2. An integrity breach – where there is an unauthorised or accidental alteration of personal data.

3. Availability breach – where there is an accidental or unauthorised loss of access to or destruction of personal data.

It is important to note that ***Personal Data Breaches*** relate solely to security incidents (whether this is a breach of a technical or an organisational security measure). Schools may breach the GDPR in other ways which do not amount to a ***Personal Data Breach***. For example, a school may breach the data protection legislation by trawling through potential job candidates' social media without notifying them that they will do so (e.g. in a privacy notice). Whilst the school may have justification to carry out the social media checks, the fact that the individual has not been informed of this processing makes it unfair and is a breach of the data protection legislation (in particular, the second data protection principle). However, as it is not a security incident that meets the definition of a ***Personal Data Breach***, it is not reportable to the ICO but should be dealt with internally through policies, training and privacy notices.

Is it mandatory to report the breach to the ICO?

As we've discussed above, the GDPR places an obligation on schools to report a ***Personal Data Breach*** to the ICO unless the personal data breach is unlikely to result in a risk to the rights of freedoms of an individual. Recital 85 of the GDPR explains that risk to rights and freedoms can include emotional distress, damage to reputation and loss of confidentiality. Therefore, it is necessary to carry out a risk assessment following any security incidents in order to determine whether or not notification is required to the Information Commissioner's Office.

Factors to consider when assessing risk

Recital 75 and 76 of the GDPR state that when assessing the risk to an individual, consideration should be given to the likelihood of there being a risk and the severity of that risk to the rights and freedoms of individuals.

The European Data Protection Board guidelines on personal data breach notification[3] recommend that the assessment of risk to an individual should take in to account the following:

3 https://ec.europa.eu/newsroom/article29/item-detail.cfm?item_id=612052

1. **The type of breach**

   Whether or not the incident can be categorised as a confidentiality breach could point towards making a self-report.

2. **The nature, sensitivities, and volume of personal data**

   A key factor to consider is the type and sensitivity of personal data that has been compromised by the ***Personal Data Breach***. The more sensitive the personal data, the higher the risk of harm will be to any of the people affected.

3. **Ease of identification of individuals**

   Another important factor to consider is how easy it will be for a party who has access to personal data to identify the specific individual involved. If for example, an encrypted laptop is lost containing highly sensitive information, the risk of the individuals being identified is reduced to almost zero and may not be notifiable to the ICO as the individuals cannot be identified.

4. **Severity of consequences for individuals**

   You will need to consider the consequences for the individuals as a result of the ***Personal Data Breach***. For example, where ***Special Categories of Personal Data*** have been disclosed, the potential damage to individuals can be severe. This is particularly clear where the breach could result in physical harm, psychological distress, humiliation or damage to reputation. If the breach contains information about vulnerable individuals, they could be placed at greater risk of harm. For example, in a number of cases, the single disclosure of someone else's address may not cause any severe consequences for the individual but in other circumstances, if a child had had been moved for their own protection and that address was then disclosed, this could cause severe consequences for that individual and therefore would require notifying the ICO.

In the case of a ***Personal Data Breach*** relating to an unauthorised disclosure, who the disclosure is made to can have a bearing on the potential risk to the individual. The EDPB Guidance states that where personal data has accidentally been disclosed to the wrong department within an organisation, "*even if the data has been accessed, the controller could still possibly trust the recipient not to take any further action with it... In such cases, this may be factored into the risk assessment following the breach. The fact that the recipient is trusted may eradicate the severity of the consequences of the breach but does not mean that a breach has not been occurred. However, this in turn may remove the likelihood of risk to individuals, thus no longer requiring notification*".

5. **Special characteristics of the individual**

Where a data breach affects the personal data of vulnerable individuals, especially children, they are at greater risk of harm or danger as a result of a ***Personal Data Breach***. This is important to consider in your risk assessment, particularly given if a data breach occurs in a school, then it is likely to affect vulnerable people including children. This will be then a factor to consider when decided whether or not the breach is reportable to the ICO.

6. **Special characteristics of the Data Controller**

The nature and the role of the ***Data Controller*** and the activities that it carries out will also affect the level of risk caused to individuals. In a school setting, you will hold a large amount of ***Special Category Personal Data*** about children and other vulnerable individuals, therefore again, this needs to be assessed when considering the risk of harm to individuals.

7. **The number of affected individuals**

Generally speaking, the larger the number of affected individuals mean that there is a greater risk of harm being caused by the breach. However, there are circumstances where a ***Personal Data Breach*** will only affect one individual and still be able to have a severe impact on that one individual depending on the nature of the personal data that has been disclosed. This therefore is another factor to consider in your risk assessment when deciding whether or not report the breach to the ICO.

Therefore, when assessing the risk that is likely to result from a ***Personal Data Breach***, the school is going to have to consider the combination of the severity of that breach on the rights of freedoms of individuals and also the likelihood of that risk occurring. The threshold of there being a risk to the rights and freedoms of the individuals is very low and therefore, if there is doubt of whether or not this risk has occurred the controller is urged to err on the side of caution and notify the ICO.

Consequences of making a self-report to the ICO

In response to a report of a ***Personal Data Breach***, the ICO may:

- Record the breach and take no further action;
- Investigate the circumstances of the breach and take any remedial action;
- Require the controller to undertake a course of action to prevent further breaches;

- Conduct onsite assessments to enter premises, access documents and interview specified persons;

- Take formal enforcement action turning such a requirement into a legal obligation; or

- Where there is a serious breach of the GDPR, the ICO may serve a monetary penalty notice up to the value of 20,000,000 Euros or 4% of annual global turnover, whichever is higher.

Action is taken by the ICO is published on its website and so can have an effect of the school's reputation. In addition to action being taken by the ICO, affected individuals now have the opportunity to claim for compensation for distress for a personal data breach. In the event of the breach affecting members of staff, the employee may also decide to raise a grievance with the HR team.

Examples of reportable breaches

- Disclosure of a child's address to an estranged parent
- Disclosure of SEN report to wrong family
- A teacher downloading pupil information and taking it with them when their employment terminates

Examples of recordable but not reportable breaches

- Lost encrypted laptop
- Letter given to wrong child but retrieved before it was opened
- Accidental deletion of records which are quickly recovered from a backup system;

Case Study – Risk Assessment Following Personal Data Breach

A secondary school asks year 11 pupils to complete a sexual health questionnaire so that the school nurse can evaluate the services being provided to the school. The questionnaire included the pupils providing details of any physical or mental illness, sexuality and sex life. The school then suffers a breach that results in the accidental disclosure of the questionnaire results to all members of staff. The DPO conducts a risk assessment upon discovering the breach to determine whether the ICO needs to be notified of the breach. The DPO concludes the breach is reportable to the ICO due to the following factors:

- It was a confidentiality breach as there was an unauthorised disclosure of personal data;
- The very nature of the information contained in the questionnaire was highly confidential and contained multiple types of ***Special Category Personal Data***;
- It would be relatively easy to identify the individuals involved due to the wide variety of information provided in the questionnaire;
- The breach is likely to cause the students involved distress, upset and embarrassment compounded by the fact that some of the students may know members of staff on a personal level (e.g. they are a relative or a family friend);
- The breach involves the personal data of children; and
- The breach involves a large number of children's personal data being disclosed and so increased the risk of harm being caused by the breach.

When to Communicate with Affected Individuals

The GDPR also places an obligation on ***Data Controllers*** to inform the individuals affected by a ***Personal Data Breach*** in certain circumstances[4]. If a breach is likely to result in a high risk to the rights and freedoms of an individual, the data controller must notify the individual without undue delay.

The threshold for notifying individuals of a breach is higher than the threshold for notifying the ICO ('risk of harm' is the threshold for reporting to the ICO whereas reporting to individuals is where there is a 'high risk of harm'). Therefore, not all breaches which are reportable to the ICO are reportable to the affected individuals. You will need to carry out an assessment to determine whether or not notification is required to the individuals affected. The same assessment as discussed in the section **'When to Notify the ICO'** above can be used.

Example of a breach reportable to affected individuals

- Taking the case study from above, a secondary school asks some year 11 pupils to complete a sexual health questionnaire so that the school nurse can evaluate the services being provided to the school. The school then suffers a breach that results in the accidental disclosure of the questionnaire results. This could cause a significant impact on the affected individuals because of the sensitivity of the information and the potential for confidential medical and sexuality details being disclosed. This is likely to result in a high risk to the rights and freedoms of the affected individuals and so they need to be informed about the breach.

Example of a breach not reportable to affected individuals

- A college accidentally deletes a record of alumni contact details. This is an "availability breach". The college is able to recover the

4 Article 34 General Data Protection Regulation (EU) 2016/679

contact details from a backup. This breach is unlikely to result in a high risk to the rights and freedoms of those individuals and they do not need to be informed about the breach.

Information to be provided

The GDPR states that specific information must be given to individuals when notifying them of a ***Personal Data Breach***. If individuals need to be informed of the breach, the school should at least provide the following information:

- A description of the nature of the breach;
- The name and contact details of the DPO or other contact point;
- A description of the likely consequences of the breach; and
- A description of the measures taken or proposed to be taken by the school to address the breach, including, where appropriate measures to mitigate its possible adverse effects.

Case Study – Notifying Individuals

Taking the example from above, the breach has arisen as a result of an error by a member of staff. The member of staff has collected the sexual health questionnaires and intended to send them as an attachment via e-mail to the school nurse. The attachment was not password protected. In error, the member of staff sent the e-mail to all staff at the school rather than the school nurse. As a minimum, the school should provide the following information to the affected pupils:

- An overview of what has happened – e.g. the sexual health questionnaires that they had completed had been sent in error to all staff at the school instead of the school nurse;

- An acknowledgement that the incident could cause them distress, upset and embarrassment;
- Details of what action the school has taken – e.g. the school has been able to delete the e-mail from its server so no one else can access the questionnaires, the school has been able to identify which members of staff accessed the questionnaires and has reminded them of their duty of confidentiality and the school will carry out more training and review its policies and procedures to ensure this will not happen again; and
- The details of the school's DPO if they wish to discuss the matter further or make a complaint.

Lessons Learned

Following any ***Personal Data Breach***, it is important to understand what lessons have been learned and what actions will be taken going forward to prevent the breach from occurring again. In any event, the ICO is likely to ask this question if you make a self-report or a complaint is made about you.

As part of your investigation into the ***Personal Data Breach***, you should be able to determine whether the breach was a result of human error or it was a more systematic issue and highlight what action can be taken to prevent the breach from occurring. This may include:

- Considering whether or not any of your policies and procedures need updating or amending;
- Considering whether any training needs have been identified; and
- Considering how effective your data breach procedure was – does it need reviewing or is any further training required?

Your lessons learned review following a ***Personal Data Breach*** should be carefully documented and any changes required implemented in a timely manner in an attempt to avoid a recurrence.

Case Study – Lessons Learned

Taking the example from above, the ***DPO*** has investigated how the breach occurred and has given consideration to what action can be taken to prevent a recurrence of the breach. The ***DPO*** concluded that the breach could have been avoided if the attachment to the e-mail had been password protected or if the e-mail had not been addressed incorrectly in the first instance. The ***DPO*** has decided that the following action needs to be taken:

- The school's data protection policies needed to be updated to highlight the importance of accuracy and ensuring e-mails are addressed correctly;
- The school's data protection policies needed to be updated to stipulate that attachments being sent via e-mail which contain ***Special Category Personal Data*** should be password protected; and
- Training should be provided to all members of staff to reinforce the importance of addressing e-mails correctly and showing staff how to password protect documents and set a delay on sending e-mails so that if an error is noticed shortly after sending, the e-mail can be recovered.

CHAPTER EIGHT
PRACTICAL EXAMPLES & SUGGESTIONS

In this chapter, we have considered some of common issues we get asked about by schools on a regular basis such as whether or not pupil information can be put on display within schools or if parents can take photographs of their children at school events. The important point to keep at the forefront of your mind is that children need particular protection when you are collecting and processing their personal data because they are less aware of the risks involved. When you process children's personal data, you should think about the need to protect them from the outset and design systems and processes with this in mind.

Displays in School

We are commonly asked whether consent is needed to display pupil's work or photographs on displays within school. The starting point is to consider what your lawful basis is to process pupil information in this way (as set out in Article 6 of the GDPR). Where you are displaying pupil work in order to improve morale within the school and/and or to promote the good work being done by pupils, your lawful basis is carrying out a public task (Article 6(e)). However, just because you have a legal justification for processing pupil information does not mean your obligations end there. You should always look to minimize any personal data that is capable of being seen from anyone outside the school itself looking in (e.g. by paying careful consideration to displays in your reception area).

The display of pupil work or photographs inside school is treated differently to publishing that pupil information outside of the school (e.g. in a magazine, brochure or in the local press). In these circumstances, consent will be the appropriate legal basis to process pupil information. Consent to publish this information will need to be obtained from either the parent or carer or the pupil, depending on their age. For further information in relation to consent please see Chapter 2 ('**The Question of Consent**').

Therefore in summary, the GDPR does not prevent you from putting pupil information on display but you should give careful consideration to whereabouts the information is being displayed and who is able to see this information. If pupil information is being used for marketing purposes (e.g. in a magazine, brochure or in a local press) then consent should be sought.

Use of Fingerprints

Many schools may have or be looking to install fingerprint recognition systems (e.g. for the payment of school meals or to take out library books). The GDPR does not prohibit the use of such systems but there are a number of considerations that need to be taken into account and a process put in place prior to the use of such a system.

Fingerprint recognition systems are classed as 'biometric data' under the GDPR as they involve specific, technical processing of the physical characteristics of an individual which confirms their identification. Biometric data is ***Special Category Personal Data*** under the GDPR. The appropriate legal basis for processing pupils' fingerprints is explicit consent (Article 6(1)(a) and Article 9(2)(a)). However, it is important to note here that the use of biometric information in schools, academies or colleges is governed by the Protection of Freedoms Act 2012, in addition to the GDPR and the Data Protection Act 2018.

The Protection of Freedoms Act 2012 states that before using a child's biometric information, the school must do the following[1]:

1 Section 26 Protection of Freedoms Act 2012

i. Notify each parent of the child of its intention to use the child's biometric information;

ii. Notify each parent that they may object to the school's use of their child's biometric information; and

iii. Obtain consent for using the child's biometric information from at least one parent.

Therefore prior to using the system, consent must be obtained from at least one parent. This consent must be obtained in writing[2]. If at any time a parent withdraws their consents or objects to the child's biometric information being used, the school must no longer process the biometric information. Whilst consent has to be obtained by at least one parent, if the child refuses to participate in or objects to the use of their biometric information, then the school must ensure that their information is not used, irrespective of any consent given by the parent of the child[3]. Where the parent (or the child) objects to the use of the system or withdraws their consent, an alternative method will need to be used instead of using the fingerprint system (e.g. a PIN number).

If you are considering installing a fingerprint recognition system, you should carry out a Data Privacy Impact Assessment (DPIA) prior to installing the system. The GDPR introduced an obligation to integrate data protection into all aspects of your data processing[4]. This is known as data protection by design and default. Article 25 of the GDPR obliges you to have regard to technical and organisational measures that will ensure compliance with the data protection principles and ensure necessary safeguards to protect personal data are integrated into the system by default. An example of this approach at work in practice is to have social media accounts automatically set to private rather than public. DPIAs are an integral part of ensuring data protection by design and default. A DPIA is an assessment for you to analyse the technology you

2 Section 27(2) Protection of Freedoms Act 2012

3 Section 26(5) Protection of Freedoms Act 2012

4 Article 25 General Data Protection Regulation (EU) 2016/679

are considering to implement and establish what harm, or potential harm, the technology poses to individual's data protection and privacy rights and what can be put in place to reduce the risk of that harm occurring.

The GDPR obliges organisations to carry out a DPIA where the processing is likely to result in a high risk to individuals. This includes where you are processing ***Special Category Personal Data*** on a large scale[5]. 'Large scale' is not defined in the GDPR but you will need to consider the number of individuals concerned and the volume of data involved. For example, in a small primary school a DPIA may not be strictly necessary but if the system was being rolled out across an entire Multi Academy Trust then it is likely to be considered to be large scale processing. Given that a fingerprint recognition system in schools would process the personal data of children (who are afforded additional protection under the GDPR) we would recommend conducting a DPIA in any event, regardless of whether or not it was strictly necessary, in order to demonstrate best practice.

Recruitment

Issues relating to recruitment and, in particular, the pre-vetting of applicants was particularly contentious in the run up to the implementation of the GDPR. Schools have a requirement to find out about criminal convictions before employing a candidate, as described in Keeping Children Safe in Education (KCSiE) 2019[6]. This requirement is fulfilled by the DBS checks that occur at the point of offering the position to a candidate. KCSIE and ICO Guidance[7] both state that pre-vetting checks should occur at the last possible moment when any offer of employment has been made to achieve data minimisation by not vetting

5 Article 35(3)(b) General Data Protection Regulation (EU) 2016/679

6 Keeping Children Safe in Education 2019 (Part Three: Safe Recruitment)

7 Section 1.6.2 ICO The Employment Practices Code

people who are not going to be offered the job anyway. However, this does not include employment history and references, which are to be obtained prior to interviewing the candidate so that any concerns raised can be explored further with the referee and then discussed with the candidate at interview[8].

Information relating to criminal offences and convictions is governed by Article 10 of the GDPR. Information of this kind was previously defined as "sensitive" data under the Data Protection Act 1998, however the GDPR has redefined it and separated from other types of sensitive data. Information about criminal convictions now has its own category under the GDPR.

In order to be able to collect and use information about criminal convictions (including conducting DBS checks and self-declaration forms), it now requires a lawful basis under Article 6 of the GDPR and a lawful basis under s.10 of the Data Protection Act 2018. The appropriate lawful basis for processing information about criminal convictions during the recruitment process under Article 6 of the GDPR is the public interest basis (Article 6(1)(e)). In addition to the lawful basis under Article 6 of the GDPR, a further legal basis needs to be established under Schedule 1 of the Data Protection Act 2018 (s.10 DPA). In the case of pre-vetting candidates in schools, there are a variety of lawful conditions to do so including:

- Preventing unlawful or detecting unlawful acts (Schedule 1, Part 2, para 10 of the DPA 2018)
- Protecting the public against dishonesty etc (Schedule 1, Part 2, para 11 of the DPA 2018)
- Safeguarding of children and of individuals at risk (Schedule 1, Part 2, para 18 of the DPA 2018)

---

8 Para 145 Keeping Children Safe in Education 2019 (Part Three: Safer Recruitment)

Whilst there are several lawful basis' for processing information about criminal convictions as part of your recruitment process, the point at which this information is collected is important. As discussed above, the pre-vetting checks should occur at the point of the offer of employment being made.

Consent has no part in this processing as it cannot be separated from getting the job. Making a job application is not the same thing as consent. Putting a question about previous convictions in an application form is not asking for consent because it is not possible to withhold consent and still go forward in the recruitment process.

Use of Personal Devices by Staff

Another common concern that was raised in the run up to the GDPR coming into force was the use of staff's own personal devices (e.g. phones, tablets and laptops) for work purposes. If managed responsibility, there are benefits in staff using their own devices as it can provide good value for money and save the school money in the long run. However, it is also important to recognise the risks posed by staff using their own devices and consider the data protection implications.

The school, as a ***Data Controller***, must ensure that its information is kept secure and confidential and have technical and organisational measures in place to prevent school information from being lost or stolen. This can be difficult to achieve if the school's information is being held by staff on their own personal e-mail accounts or saved on their own laptop. Staff's own devices may not be subject to the same level of security as school equipment (e.g. personal e-mail accounts are not secure and can be hacked relatively easily or infected with malware). This means that if the device is lost, stolen or hacked into, school information could easily be accessed or used unlawfully.

The GDPR does not ban the use of personal devices for work purposes but if it is something staff in your school use, you need to take steps to address the data protection implications. A policy should be put in place to govern the use of personal devices for work purposes. It should include appropriate security measures that need to be in place before staff can use their personal devices for work purposes. These measures may include:

- Ensuring the device is password protected and it has an automatic lock to help protect the device when it is not in use;
- Ensuring the device software is up to date;
- Activating and use anti-virus protection;
- Installing remote wiping software so that the device can be wiped in the event that it is lost or stolen;
- Ensuring all school information is removed from the device before the device is disposed of or the member of staff leaves the school.

Once an appropriate policy has been formulated, you will need to make all members of staff aware of the policy and provide training where necessary to ensure that it is understood.

The use of personal devices by staff for work purposes all raises the risk of school information being used for different purposes from which it was originally collected. In one case a former head teacher was prosecuted by the ICO for saving pupil information onto a personal USB stick whilst he was working at one primary school and then subsequently uploading the pupil information onto a server at a new primary school without a lawful reason to do so[9]. Having a process in place to ensure any personal devices are wiped of school information at

9 https://ico.org.uk/about-the-ico/news-and-events/news-and-blogs/2018/12/former-headteacher-prosecuted-for-unlawfully-obtaining-school-children-s-personal-information/

the time staff members leave would assist in reducing the risk of this happening in the future.

Signing in and Access Control

Physical security controls to the school premises play a keep part in your data protection compliance as well as ensuring the safeguarding of children by preventing unauthorised access to the premises. As physical security measures (such as secure entrances) prevent school premises from being accessed from unauthorised visitors they will count towards your GDPR compliance.

In addition, any use of CCTV will enhance security at the school. The ICO has produced extensive guidance relating to the use of CCTV[10]. CCTV usage must be communicated to the individuals being recorded. The most effective way of doing this is by using prominently placed signs at the entrance to the school premises and reinforcing this with further signs inside the school. Clear and prominent signs are particularly important where the surveillance systems are very discreet.

Visitor signing-in books contain personal information and so the GDPR applies to their use. The book and the information within it must be kept secure so that the information is not accessed by people unauthorised to see it. This should also include ensuring that previous entries are not visible to other visitors.

Taking Photographs in Schools

There is a common misconception that you cannot take photographs of children in schools for data protection reasons. There may be a number of reasons why you want to prevent the use of photography in school but data protection is unlikely to be the concern. The ICO regularly

10 https://ico.org.uk/media/1542/cctv-code-of-practice.pdf

publishes guidance refuting the myth that the DPA prohibits the use of photography.

Photos taken by parents for their own personal use are exempt from the DPA and the GDPR and so the legislation does not apply. For example if a parent takes photographs of sports day or the school nativity to put in the family photo album, the DPA or the GDPR will not apply as the photographs are for personal use.

The position is different however if photographs are being taken for marketing or media purposes (e.g. to be published in a school prospectus or the local newspaper). In these circumstances, the GDPR and the DPA does apply and consent will be required from either the parent or carer or the pupil, depending on their age. For further information in relation to consent please see Chapter 2 ('**The Question of Consent**').

Keeping Old Photographs

In some circumstances, you may be able to justify keeping older photos, or those of particular historical interest, under the 'public interest' basis. This means you will not need GDPR standard consent to store the photos, provided that all you are doing with them is storing them.

This approach will apply if you are archiving the photos in the public interest or for historical research purposes. Archived photos are those stored in areas which are not easily accessible to the public, such as school offices or filing cabinets. It will not apply to photos kept in places such as reception areas, school corridors or on a website, because this would amount to marketing and would require consent.

In order to determine which photos can be archived in the public interest, and therefore be held under the public interest legal basis, your governors and your ***DPO*** should meet to agree a standardised procedure for keeping photographs.

This procedure should set out which photos can be kept in the public interest, and to which another lawful basis would need to apply to retain them. As well as the public or historical research interest in keeping a photo, the procedure should consider whether the individuals depicted are likely to be distressed by the photo being kept for archiving purposes, as potentially damaging photographs should not be kept. You should document the decisions taken here when setting up this procedure to use as evidence if these practices are later questioned.

When deciding upon the procedure, consider:

- Age: the older the photos are, the easier it will be justify their presence in an archive (note: where it can be shown that they depict no living individuals, the photo is not personal data in any event);
- The number of people in photos: photos of individuals, rather than large groups or classes, will usually have less reason to be in an archive, as there is less public or historical interest in individual photos;
- Setting: a whole-school photo taken in front of the school building is far more likely to be of historical importance and therefore worthy of archiving in the public interest than a snap of a small group of children in a classroom.

Post

The use of postal mail in schools is another area where we are often asked to advise. The GDPR places an obligation on schools to ensure that appropriate security measures are in place to prevent personal information being lost or disclosed in error. The use of postal mail for sending sensitive documents needs to be considered carefully due to the risks of post being incorrectly addressed or going missing. Ultimately, whether or not school information can be sent in the post will largely depend on the level of sensitivity of the information and the potential impact on the school and/or the individual concerned if the information was lost or disclosed to an unauthorised person.

If the letter/document you wish to send contains personal data but does not contain ***Special Category Personal Data*** (for example information about health or disability) it could potentially be sent in the post if you consider that this is the most appropriate method of sending. Where the letter or document contains ***Special Category Personal Data***, this needs to be treated with a greater degree of care and should not be sent by non-recorded post as there is a risk of the post being lost or the document being opened by the wrong person. A more appropriate method would be to send the document as an encrypted (e.g. password protected) attachment to a verified e-mail address or by hand delivery.

Another potential issue faced by the use of post is whether or not there is a procedure in place for post to be opened during the school holidays. Since the GDPR introduced a shorter time period to respond to subject access requests (1 month), the school may face a complaint if a subject access request is received during the school holidays and is not responded to within the statutory 1 month time frame (see Chapter 3 for further details on subject access requests).

Parents' Evenings

The administration of parents' evenings can be a large task for a school to undertake. Schools may choose to use an online system to make and manage parents' evening bookings. The provider delivering such an online system is likely to be a ***Data Processor*** and therefore you will need to ensure that there is a written contract in place with the provider which details the technical and organisational measures that are in place to protect the school's information. This may be incorporated into the provider's terms and conditions. For further information, please see Chapter 5 '**Data Processors**'.

On the actual date of the parents' evening, the school will also need to ensure its signing in books and the information within it are kept secure so that the information is not accessed by people unauthorised to see it. This should also include ensuring that previous entries are not visible to other visitors.

Governors

The school, as the ***Data Controller***, is responsible for ensuring it complies with the GDPR, acting through the school's leadership team, the ***DPO*** (if applicable) and the board of governors.

Governors need to be aware that the GDPR also applies to their use of school information. As discussed earlier, the school as a ***Data Controller*** must ensure that its information is kept secure and confidential and have technical and organisational measures in place to prevent school information from being lost or stolen. This can be difficult to achieve if the school's information is being held by governors on their own personal e-mail accounts or saved on their own laptop. If school information is being sent to governors and it contains personal information, care must be taken to ensure the e-mail address is accurate and up-to-date and any attachment should be encrypted (e.g. password protected). Any paper copies of documents containing personal information should not be left unattended and will need to be disposed of confidentially (e.g. placed in the school's confidential waste). For further details about use of personal devices, please see the section '*Use of Personal Devices by Staff*' above.

APPENDIX A
SUPPLIER DATA PROTECTION COMPLIANCE QUESTIONNAIRE

SUPPLIER NAME ....

IMPORTANT NOTE

We take our responsibilities of protecting the privacy of our students, parents/carers and workforce very seriously. As one of our suppliers you will be processing the personal data of our students, parents/carers and/or employees. By processing personal data we mean any one or more of the following: collecting, viewing, recording, storing, organising, filing, sharing, deleting, editing or archiving personal information.

As you are processing the personal data of our students, parents/carers and/or workforce please complete the questionnaire below. The questionnaire has been devised by us as a preliminary assessment of your compliance with data protection legislation. On completion, we will review the answers you have provided and determine whether any further steps are required. Please answer the questions honestly as we aim to work with our suppliers to ensure we comply with data protection legislation and any deliberately false information provided may be a breach of your contract with us.

Please provide a detailed response to each question. If any of the questions do not relate to your supply of goods and services to us, please mark the question as "N/A" and provide an explanation. If you are unable to complete all the answers by [DATE] please mark on the question that further information is to follow and return the questionnaire to us. Any outstanding information can be sent to us at a later date.

Part One: Compliance with Data Protection Policies

No.	Question	Supplier Response
1.	Do you have a documented Data Protection Policy which obliges your organisation and all its employees and/or contractors to comply with Data Protection legislation?	
2.	How often is your Data Protection Policy reviewed?	
3.	Who is responsible for the circulation, maintenance and development of your Data Protection Policy?	
4.	Is your Data Protection Policy readily available to all users? If yes, please state where it is located.	
5.	Do you have a documented Information Security Policy which obliges your organisation and all its employees and/or contractors to comply with Data Protection legislation?	

6.	How often is your Information Security Policy reviewed?	
7.	Who is responsible for the circulation, maintenance and development of your Information Security Policy?	
8.	Is your Information Security Policy readily available to all users? If yes, please state where it is located.	
9.	Is a complete set of your data protection and security policies available for review?	

Part Two: Security Control

No.	Question	Supplier Response
1.	Describe the technological security measures you have in place to safeguard personal data.	
2.	Do you hold an information management security standards accreditation (e.g. ISO 27001)?	
3.	Have your security policies, procedures and standards been reviewed and assessed by a qualified independent organisation?	
4.	Has your security infrastructure been reviewed and tested by a qualified independent organisation?	
5.	How are your systems protected against newly discovered vulnerabilities or threats?	
6.	Are your security policies and procedures routinely tested?	

Part Three: Environmental, Physical and Organisational Security

No.	Question	Supplier Response
1.	How many members of staff will have access to our data?	
2.	Are background verification checks carried out on employees and contractors who have access to our data?	
3.	Where your staff have access to our data, is there a confidentiality clause in their employment contracts?	
4.	Do you offer regular data protection training to all your staff?	
5.	Do you maintain a record of any data protection training provided to your staff?	
6.	Do you have a documented procedure for dealing with members of staff who breach any of your data protection policies?	

7.	Describe what physical security measures you have in place for unauthorised access to any of your workspace (i.e key fob/ID card)?	
8.	What measures do you have in place to prevent staff from installing potentially malicious software?	
9.	How do you protect information that is taken offsite?	
11.	Do you have an Access Control policy (i.e. only certain members of staff can access certain information)?	
12.	Do you use any sub-contractors in the delivery of your service to us? If yes, does your contract include a provision in relation to your respective data protection obligations?	

Part Four: Data Breaches

No.	Question	Supplier Response
1.	Do you have a documented procedure which details a plan of action in the event of a breach of data protection legislation?	
2.	Do you have a procedure in place to ensure we are notified without delay of a data breach concerning the personal data of our customers, tenants and/or employees?	
3.	After a data breach, are your policies and procedures reviewed to determine if any modifications need to be made?	
4.	Have you breached data protection legislation in the last 3 years where the breach was reported to the Information Commissioner? If yes, please provide details and explain what action was taken.	

Part Five: Data Retention and Disposal

No.	Question	Supplier Response
1.	Do you have a Data Retention policy?	
2.	Describe how our data is permanently deleted once it is no longer required in order for you to fulfil your contractual obligations.	
3.	How do you dispose of digital media when it is no longer in use?	
4.	Do you keep a log of the disposal of digital media?	

Signed:..

Dated:...

Print name:..

Position:...

APPENDIX B
PERSONAL DATA BREACH CHECKLIST

Name	
Position	
Contact details	
Date	
Time/date of breach	
Time/date breach discovered	
Description of information involved	[Detail as much information as possible—including the number of people involved, the type of information and the sensitivity]
Summary of incident	[Give a detailed account of what happened]

Is breach ongoing?	YES / NO
What steps have been taken to minimise the effects of the breach?	[Detail any steps taken to rectify the breach e.g. e-mail recall]
Parties affected by the breach	[List the individuals affected by the breach]
Signed:	
Name:	
Position:	
Date:	

'A Practical Guide to Noise Induced Hearing Loss (NIHL) Claims' by Andrew Mckie, Ian Skeate, Gareth McAloon

'An Introduction to Beauty Negligence Claims – A Practical Guide for the Personal Injury Practitioner' by Greg Almond

'Intercompany Agreements for Transfer Pricing Compliance' by Paul Sutton

'Zen and the Art of Mediation' by Martin Plowman

'A Practical Guide to the SRA Principles, Individual and Law Firm Codes of Conduct 2019 – What Every Law Firm Needs to Know' by Paul Bennett

'A Practical Guide to Licensing Law for Commercial Property Lawyers' by Niall McCann & Richard Williams

'A Practical Guide to Adoption for Family Lawyers' by Graham Pegg

'Essential Motor Finance Law for the Busy Practitioner' by Richard Humphreys

'A Practical Guide to Industrial Disease Claims' by Andrew Mckie & Ian Skeate

'A Practical Guide to the Law of Armed Conflict' by Jo Morris & Libby Anderson

'A Practical Guide to Redundancy' by Philip Hyland

'A Practical Guide to Vicarious Liability' by Mariel Irvine

'A Practical Guide to Claims Arising from Delays in Diagnosing Cancer' by Bella Webb

'A Practical Guide to Applications for Landlord's Consent and Variation of Leases' by Mark Shelton

'A Practical Guide to Relief from Sanctions Post-Mitchell and Denton' by Peter Causton

'Butler's Equine Tax Planning: 2nd Edition' by Julie Butler

'A Practical Guide to Equity Release for Advisors' by Paul Sams

'A Practical Guide to Unlawful Eviction and Harassment' by Stephanie Lovegrove

'A Practical Guide to the Law Relating to Food' by Ian Thomas

'A Practical Guide to the Ending of Assured Shorthold Tenancies' by Elizabeth Dwomoh

'A Practical Guide to Financial Services Claims' by Chris Hegarty

'The Law of Houses in Multiple Occupation: A Practical Guide to HMO Proceedings' by Julian Hunt

'A Practical Guide to Unlawful Eviction and Harassment' by Stephanie Lovegrove

'A Practical Guide to Solicitor and Client Costs' by Robin Dunne
'A Practical Guide to Wrongful Conception, Wrongful Birth and Wrongful Life Claims' by Rebecca Greenstreet
'Occupiers, Highways and Defective Premises Claims: A Practical Guide Post-Jackson – 2nd Edition' by Andrew Mckie
'A Practical Guide to Financial Ombudsman Service Claims' by Adam Temple & Robert Scrivenor
'A Practical Guide to the Law of Enfranchisement and Lease Extension' by Paul Sams
'A Practical Guide to Marketing for Lawyers – 2nd Edition' by Catherine Bailey & Jennet Ingram
'A Practical Guide to Advising Schools on Employment Law' by Jonathan Holden
'Certificates of Lawful Use and Development: A Guide to Making and Determining Applications' by Bob Mc Geady & Meyric Lewis
'A Practical Guide to the Law of Dilapidations' by Mark Shelton
'A Guide to Consent in Clinical Negligence Post-Montgomery' by Lauren Sutherland QC
'A Practical Guide to Running Housing Disrepair and Cavity Wall Claims: 2nd Edition' by Andrew Mckie & Ian Skeate
'A Practical Guide to Digital and Social Media Law for Lawyers' by Sherree Westell
'A Practical Guide to Holiday Sickness Claims – 2nd Edition' by Andrew Mckie & Ian Skeate
'A Practical Guide to Elderly Law' by Justin Patten
'Arguments and Tactics for Personal Injury and Clinical Negligence Claims' by Dorian Williams
'A Practical Guide to QOCS and Fundamental Dishonesty' by James Bentley
'A Practical Guide to Drone Law' by Rufus Ballaster, Andrew Firman, Eleanor Clot
'A Practical Guide to Compliance for Personal Injury Firms Working With Claims Management Companies' by Paul Bennett
'A Practical Guide to the Landlord and Tenant Act 1954: Commercial Tenancies' by Richard Hayes & David Sawtell
'A Practical Guide to Psychiatric Claims in Personal Injury' by Liam Ryan
'A Practical Guide to Dog Law for Owners and Others' by Andrea Pitt

'RTA Allegations of Fraud in a Post-Jackson Era: The Handbook – 2nd Edition' by Andrew Mckie
'RTA Personal Injury Claims: A Practical Guide Post-Jackson' by Andrew Mckie
'On Experts: CPR35 for Lawyers and Experts' by David Boyle
'An Introduction to Personal Injury Law' by David Boyle
'A Practical Guide to Claims Arising From Accidents Abroad and Travel Claims' by Andrew Mckie & Ian Skeate
'A Practical Guide to Chronic Pain Claims' by Pankaj Madan
'A Practical Guide to Claims Arising from Fatal Accidents' by James Patience
'A Practical Approach to Clinical Negligence Post-Jackson' by Geoffrey Simpson-Scott
'Employers' Liability Claims: A Practical Guide Post-Jackson' by Andrew Mckie
'A Practical Guide to Subtle Brain Injury Claims' by Pankaj Madan
'A Practical Guide to Costs in Personal Injury Cases' by Matthew Hoe
'The No Nonsense Solicitors' Practice: A Guide To Running Your Firm' by Bettina Brueggemann
'The Queen's Counsel Lawyer's Omnibus: 20 Years of Cartoons from The Times 1993-2013' by Alex Steuart Williams

These books and more are available to order online direct from the publisher at www.lawbriefpublishing.com, where you can also read free sample chapters. For any queries, contact us on 0844 587 2383 or mail@lawbriefpublishing.com.

Our books are also usually in stock at www.amazon.co.uk with free next day delivery for Prime members, and at good legal bookshops such as Wildy & Sons.

We are regularly launching new books in our series of practical day-to-day practitioners' guides. Visit our website and join our free newsletter to be kept informed and to receive special offers, free chapters, etc.

You can also follow us on Twitter at www.twitter.com/lawbriefpub.

Printed in Great Britain
by Amazon

35339607R00066